And He Did Hide Himself

And He Did Hide Himself

A Play in Four Acts

by

IGNAZIO SILONE

Translated from the Italian by

DARINA LARACY

These things spake Jesus and departed,
and did hide himself from them

JOHN XII. 36

JONATHAN CAPE
THIRTY BEDFORD SQUARE
LONDON

FIRST PUBLISHED 1946
JONATHAN CAPE LTD.   30 BEDFORD SQUARE, LONDON
AND 91 WELLINGTON STREET WEST, TORONTO

PRINTED IN GREAT BRITAIN IN THE CITY OF OXFORD
AT THE ALDEN PRESS
BOUND BY A. W. BAIN & CO. LTD., LONDON

TO THE READER

THE characters of this drama are men of to-day, but they 'come from far and are going far'. They belong only incidentally to the chronicle of time. Their existence bears witness to the spiritual journey of the author and, together with him, a considerable number of men of his generation, in these last years.

The author, whose starting-point was the representation of a certain contemporary society, was drawn by painful degrees to search into its structure. The most notable thing about this society is its antiquity: customs, characters, castes, essential institutions have all remained those of classical comedy and tragedy.

In modern drama there intervenes, in the guise of a protagonist, a new element: the proletarian. Not new in the sense that he was unknown to antiquity; but his hardships and his destiny were not then held to be the stuff of history, thought or art. If the condition of this personage appears to us moderns the closest to human truth it is because, between the ancients and us, there has come Jesus Christ.

In all these two thousand years the Christian revolution has not succeeded in destroying the classical human relationships of ancient comedy and tragedy, but it has enabled us to judge them from a radically new standpoint. In the Middle Ages this judgment was personified by the saints and martyrs, but for some time past it would seem as if the men who 'hunger and thirst after righteousness' had 'gone out of the temple'. None the less it is they who carry within themselves the truth of Christ.

The rediscovery of a Christian heritage in the revolution of our time remains the most important gain that has been made in these last years for the conscience of our generation.

In a work entitled *Atto di rinascita* the author has already summed up this event in the following terms: 'Modern Socialism, after the first World War, fared like the hunter who set out to hunt quails and fell among wolves. In the unforeseen combat with the wolves those Socialists were saved who were not only electors and tax-payers but also whole, real and entire men. In the combat with the wolves Socialism, to save itself, has gone beyond the narrow boundaries of the bourgeois spirit and has rediscovered its Christian ancestry. Suffering has carved out new dimensions in our souls, of which we were unaware in 1919.'

It is a heritage weighed down with debts. A living, painful, almost absurd heritage. In the sacred history of man on earth, it is still, alas, Good Friday. Men who 'hunger and thirst after righteousness' are still derided, persecuted, put to death. The spirit of man is still forced to save itself in hiding.

The revolution of our epoch, promoted by politicians and economists, thus takes on the form of a 'sacred mystery', with the very fate of man on earth for theme.

The tasks of the economic and political order are by no means obscured or hidden thereby; they are indeed the first and main tasks. But the men called on to carry them out must know that they come from far and are going far.

IGNAZIO SILONE

Baden, Switzerland
August 15*th*, 1944

And He Did Hide Himself

CHARACTERS

PIETRO SPINA (*also* DON PAOLO SPADA)
ANNINA, *betrothed to*
LUIGI MURICA, *student, son of*
DANIELE MURICA, *farmer*
BROTHER GIOACCHINO, *mendicant friar*
ROMEO, *factory worker*
ULIVA
CICALA, *knife grinder*
NUNZIO SACCA, *doctor*
DON MARCO TUGLIO-ZABAGLIA, *otherwise* ZABAGLIONE,
   orator
AGOSTINO ⎫
DONATO   ⎬ *peasants*
MATTEO   ⎭
The LANDLADY *at Fossa*
The LANDLADY *at Pietrasecca*
Various VILLAGE NOTABLES, *a* SCRIBE, PIOUS WOMEN,
    some PEASANTS *and their* WIVES, *a* REPROBATE
    WOMAN, *a* LITTLE BOY

This play was inspired by the author's novel *Bread and Wine*

The action takes place in Italy, in a region of the Abruzzi mountains called the Marsica, during the autumn of 1935. *The names of the villages are fictitious*

ACT I

The dimly lit interior of an old stable for donkeys. In the centre of the back wall there is a wide rustic single door; in the left-hand wall there is a smaller door, with an opening which serves as a window. The wooden roof of the stable is supported by two tree trunks acting as pillars; on the tree trunks hang ropes, bridles, harness; from the roof hangs an oil lamp that has gone out. Along the entire length of the right-hand wall runs the manger, also made of wood; at the back, to the right, part of the manger is cut off by a wooden partition about three and a half feet high, reaching to the middle of the stable; a donkey leans its head and neck out over the partition; it is the only animal in the stable. In the right-hand corner, behind the wooden partition, stands a ladder which leads through a trap-door in the roof to the hayloft. The litters of the absent donkeys are strewn with clean straw. Placed side by side along the left-hand wall there are two donkey's pack-saddles, a vat, some tools: rakes, pitchforks, poles. It is morning.

SCENE 1

AGOSTINO, DONATO, MATTEO

(AGOSTINO, *the owner of the stable, climbs down the ladder from the hayloft and begins scattering straw on the floor with a pitchfork;* MATTEO *and* DONATO *enter cautiously by the door at the back and close it behind them. All three have the rough and squalid appearance of poor peasants; they are dressed as poor peasants dress the world over, without any trace of traditional peasant dress; their age is uncertain, between forty-five and sixty years.* DONATO *posts himself at the closed door in the left-hand wall and keeps an*

attentive watch through the little window.
MATTEO *makes a survey of the stable, looks
into the manger, under the pack-saddles and
then stops, hesitant and deferential, in front of
the donkey whose head emerges above the wooden
partition*)

MATTEO Is this him? (*He asks turning to* AGOSTINO
*feigning gravity and surprise, with the clumsy gestures
of a clown*) Is this the one they've been telling us about
this many a long day and who arrived last night? Greet-
ings to you, comrade donkey. (*He makes a bow*) I am
Matteo, allow me to introduce myself. I am – but this
is between ourselves – comrade Matteo; and fifteen
years ago, in the days when we took the land, I had the
honour of carrying the red standard of redemption in
the processions of the people; and as everyone can tell
you, my arms never faltered in holding on high the
banner of our hope, not even when the north wind
blew nor when the cowardly hirelings of our masters,
with the rabble of armed men to back them, would
fall on us with sticks or stones. And the other one
over there, who came with me, is Donato, and in
those days – but this is between ourselves – he was
comrade Donato. And his voice was the strongest and
the most resounding in the red processions of those
days, when the peasants would intone the hymns of
the new faith. And since then he has never sung
again, as everyone knows. And the other is Agostino,
and there was a time – but this is between ourselves –
when he was comrade Agostino, and in those days . . .
DONATO (*leaving the window and turning to* AGOSTINO)
Barletta said to tell you he's not coming because he has
his maize. And Salvatore said to tell you he's not coming because he has his vine. And Luca won't be coming, he said to tell you, because to his mind it would be

madness to come. And he also said to tell you that he's long past the age of twenty, as we know, and that he has a wife and children, as we know, and that his name must on no account be mentioned.

AGOSTINO I'm much obliged to you for coming, Donato. Did anyone see you on the road?

DONATO I've come, Agostino, solely because you sent for me. Just as you would have come if I had sent for you. But I too, as everyone knows, am a long way past the age of twenty. And madness, as everyone knows, is no longer to my fancy either. After all that has happened, Agostino, and that everyone knows, we shouldn't even speak of such things any more.

MATTEO (*in an undertone, turning impatiently to* AGOSTINO) Well, where is Don Pietro Spina, or rather, though it seems a bit queer to me to call him so, and I have to make an effort to say it, where is comrade Pietro Spina? If I've understood you rightly, Agostino, he's the one who was supposed to have been coming all this time and who eventually arrived last night, and has things to tell us? I don't know him personally, but I've heard tell of him.

DONATO (*interrupting*) But wasn't he in foreign parts? At least so they said. And what has he come back for now? And what in the devil's name does he want from us?

AGOSTINO (*signing to the others to lower their voices still more*) You know, the Spinas have always been a bit mad. Now I don't mean bad, but mad. If it wasn't horses it was women, if it wasn't women it was the Church, if it wasn't one thing it was another; they have always been a bit mad, all of them. You know that as well as I do. If folks don't know them, they know about them. But this one, as you'll see for yourselves, this one has got hold of an entirely new craze, a strange kind of madness for one that's rich.

DONATO (*irritably*) Yes, to be sure, I can see that well enough, when you're rich it may be useful, it may even be diverting to act crazy; and if they get tired of the old crazes, I can see well enough that the rich have to keep thinking of new ones to make the time pass. But what does he want with us now? Didn't he have the good luck to be away in foreign parts? What can have brought him back to this unfortunate country?

MATTEO (*highly alarmed, to* AGOSTINO) Is he raving mad, did you say, or just touched?

AGOSTINO He got here last night on foot, he told me. He had been walking for four or five hours in the pelting rain, so as to dodge the police at the railway stations he said. And he was drenched to the skin, soaking and spattered with mud like a drowned rat, and he was burning with fever and his teeth were chattering and he was trembling so much, he couldn't stand on his feet. The moment I saw who it was, I wanted to put him up at our place, as was only natural, and as any Christian in my shoes would have done. And my wife too, when she found out who he was, and that he was a Spina, she begged and besought him to take shelter with us, as was only natural. But you might as well speak to the wind, he wouldn't give in, he said the armed men were after him, and he had narrowly escaped arrest twice yesterday, and he said he didn't want to compromise anybody, and all our pleading was to no purpose. If they were to find him in the hayloft he told me he'd pretend he crept in there unknown to me.

DONATO If they were to find us all here together with him, maybe he thinks he wouldn't be getting us into trouble? And what sense would there be in it anyhow?

AGOSTINO He wanted me to send for you, that's all.

14

He insisted, and he said he had come back from foreign parts just for that and for no other reason. And he knows that some day or other he may be arrested, he said, so he has no time to lose. And he made me send for you this very morning, that's all.

DONATO Didn't you tell him about our tribulations? Didn't you say to him that none of us dare put a foot inside the other's house nowadays, lest we rouse the suspicions of the neighbours? Didn't you tell him that we take good care not to find ourselves in the same tavern Saturday nights, and that even at Sunday Mass we're careful not to kneel beside one another, so as not to rouse suspicion?

MATTEO Friendship has become a mortal sin, and folks that know each other and trust each other and would like to be together, can't be together any more. But they're not allowed to be alone either. The lambs and wolves must run together.

DONATO Didn't you explain to him what a miserable plight we're in?

AGOSTINO What explaining could I do to a man in that condition? He was born hereabouts, he's a scholar, and if it weren't for certain things that he just won't stand for, he wouldn't need any explaining. When he speaks, I have a feeling that he's seeing things we don't see, and the things we see he doesn't see at all, that's my feeling.

DONATO So to your mind he's really mad?

MATTEO (*in alarm, to* AGOSTINO) Is he raving mad, or just touched?

AGOSTINO Maybe he's not a real madman at all, maybe he's something entirely different, the very opposite of mad; but I don't know how to explain it to you. (*Footsteps are heard overhead.* AGOSTINO *signs to the others to be silent*) He's awake now, he'll be coming down.

SCENE 2

The ABOVE, *and* PIETRO SPINA

> (PIETRO SPINA *comes briskly down the ladder and walks over, resolute and smiling, with outstretched hands, towards the three; his age is indefinable: his face, emaciated and worn by suffering, is that of a man who has reached maturity, but his bearing, his gestures, his mop of hair, his voice are those of a youth; he is poorly dressed, without collar or tie; but it is clear, from various details of his appearance, that he is an intellectual and of gentle birth. The exceptional intensity of his internal state is evident mainly from his way of looking at people)*

MATTEO (*approaching* SPINA, *ceremonious and awkward*) I am Matteo, or as I might say comrade Matteo. It was I, so to speak, that used to carry the flag, as everyone can tell you. And this is Donato, of course, comrade Donato, who used to sing, and since then he has never sung any more, as everyone can tell you.

SPINA (*to* AGOSTINO) And the others?

AGOSTINO (*evasively*) One of them said he'd got to attend to his maize, another to his vine, another to his home affairs.

SPINA (*firmly*) It doesn't matter if there are only a few of us to start with. The others will come. Forgive me, have you been waiting long? Agostino, you should have wakened me the moment these two comrades arrived. I'm sorry to have kept you waiting. I'm not lazy, you know; but one can sleep so soundly on the floor, on the straw.

DONATO To be sure, we all know that; if you sleep on the floor you don't fall out of bed.

MATTEO (*taking* SPINA *aside*) Did you mean that about sleeping on straw? I've got a special reason for asking you. (*Whispering*) Could I offer you a real bargain? A bargain for you, naturally. I'll give you a cartload of straw and in exchange you'll give me a few woollen mattresses, with bedclothes for each, of course, after all, they're of no use to you.

SPINA (*turning to all three*) My friends, I can't tell you how glad I am to be here with you at last. I was abroad and I've come home just for this.

DONATO (*incredulous*) Just to be with us?

SPINA To live and fight at your side.

MATTEO Do you think you'll get anything out of it?

SPINA A great deal.

MATTEO I don't want to disillusion you, but I'd better tell you straight that the only things you're likely to get out of being with us are fleas.

SPINA I can tell you this: the little I know, I did not learn at the university; I learned it in the company of men like you. And if my life has a purpose, I found it through contact with men like you. My whole being has now come to need that contact as vitally as my lungs need air. I'm also convinced, however, that this free and voluntary way of standing by each other in danger is most necessary for you too. No one can be completely a man if he's all alone, or in unwilling company. Because brotherhood is the sacred truth of man. That has come to be a forbidden truth in this country of ours nowadays: the order that's being imposed on us is based on utter contempt for man. But if you maim a man by depriving him of brotherhood, he becomes a tree without roots or branches, a sterile plant. A people of despised, distrustful, humiliated men and women is a pestilent swamp. Cowardice, envy, suspicion, selfishness and treachery flourish in it as mosquitoes do in swamps. Either we rediscover the brotherhood of man, or we perish. My friends, I've come to tell you this: it's essential, it's imperative that we come together, put ourselves together, and build up, here in this country, living cells of men who are complete, that is to say fraternal; we must defend ourselves from the contagion of death. I tell you, it's desperately urgent. In a few days' time, as you're possibly aware, the new war is going to break out in Africa, and what a cold-blooded cynical infamous war it's going to be. Contempt for man is going to celebrate its triumph. The most effective protest we could make would be, not a noisy individual act of terrorism, but an act of friendship, an act of brotherhood. Let me say it to you once more: I've come back from abroad for this, and this alone. Not by any means to command you, but to be together with you. (*To* DONATO *and* MATTEO) Perhaps you didn't know that I belong to this part of the country too?

(DONATO, MATTEO *and* AGOSTINO *exchange embarrassed glances*)

DONATO (*overcoming his hesitation*) Young man, I'm sorry to interrupt, but as you'll see it's not really an interruption, in a way, in fact it's an answer to what you've been saying to us. Well, here's my question: How old is the world? As you're a scholar, so to speak, maybe you can tell us what the Scripture says.

SPINA (*smiling and docile*) Well, according to the Bible, the world is about six thousand years old; according to some men of science . . .

DONATO All right, let's say the world is six thousand years old. Now, young man, that desperate state of things you've been talking about just now is six thousand years old too, and you'd do well to bear it in mind. For the last six thousand years the brotherhood of man has been trampled under foot.

MATTEO (*repeating*) For six thousand years. (*To* SPINA) If you've got paper and pencil, you'd do well to make a note of it, so as not to forget. A six and then a lot of noughts.

AGOSTINO For six thousand years the poor have been poor, despised, humiliated, offended, that's God's truth.

SPINA (*vehemently*) That's not quite true; but what if it were? It's not quite true, I tell you, that men have always been unhappy, humiliated, downtrodden and exploited *in the same way;* but all right, what if it were true? Why shouldn't it be possible to have done with it once and for all? Isn't the struggle to be free — just think this over — isn't the struggle to be free already, in itself, a kind of freedom?

(AGOSTINO, DONATO *and* MATTEO a*gain steal embarrassed glances at each other*)

DONATO Of course, in its own way, madness is freedom too.

AGOSTINO And dreaming too, in a way, is undoubtedly freedom.

MATTEO In those days, when I used to carry the flag, I often used to dream at night that my donkey could fly. It was beautiful to see.

DONATO In those strange days, I too used to dream, like the others, and indeed I liked best to dream with my eyes open. I used to sing, and dream of wolves and lambs feeding together, and State employees who didn't rob, and orators who didn't lie, and priests who really believed in God. For those sacrilegious dreams our lords and masters had us beaten up and made us drink castor oil; and besides, when all's said and done, I'm past twenty now, I'm past wanting to sing, and I'm also past hankering after the impossible.

AGOSTINO (*to* MATTEO *who is standing by the door with the little window*) Look out, Matteo, see if anyone is hanging around.

SPINA (*approaching the donkey; in a voice veiled with sadness*) And what about you, dear old comrade donkey, do you reason, or rather do you feel in the same way as your master? Yes, it's more than likely that you too, humble and patient comrade, thrashed and goaded comrade, it's even natural that you, for six thousand years a prisoner of the same destiny, should feel as hopeless as they do, and that you cannot imagine any other existence but this.

But there's more excuse for you. I don't say this to offend you, please believe me, but all the same I think there's more excuse for you.

AGOSTINO (*with an abrupt movement of pity, to* SPINA) I can't tell you how sorry I am, Pietro, but we simply had to let you know how things are here, we couldn't deceive you. No doubt you're very disappointed in us now, Pietro, after that long journey, after those hardships and those dangers, you must be discouraged now, and may be, too, there's bitterness in your heart against us.

DONATO (*to* AGOSTINO) Why, none of us sent for him, he came to us of his own accord; so it's no concern of ours.

MATTEO And it's not as if he didn't have the money for his journeying; so it's really no concern of ours.

AGOSTINO (*to* SPINA) Now listen; Pietro, if you'll give me leave, I'd like very much to talk to you as if you were my son. You know, I knew your father – may his soul rest in peace – and as a lad, before you were born, I served in your house, I worked on your land and I'm old enough to be your father. So you must allow me to put in a word. Who's forcing you to ruin your life the way you're doing? Instead of sleeping on straw and in ditches and risking your health, which doesn't seem any too strong to me, and hiding from the police as though you were an evildoer, why for the love of Christ don't you go home? Your grandmother and your uncles still have great influence, you know that as well as I do, and they could easily get a pardon for you.

SPINA (*smiles*) Don't you worry about me, Agostino. I should be a man of little faith if I were to give up hope because of what you said to me just now. Ah, I know that the greatest strength, perhaps the only strength of tyrants lies in the resigned and frightened souls of their slaves. You mustn't mind my talking like this, but I know well enough that I'll have trouble in making myself understood. Just as it's difficult to speak of colours to the blind, so I realize it's uphill work talking about freedom and dignity to men that feel no need of them.

MATTEO (*interrupts, conciliatory and complimentary*) With the learning you've got and this fine power of speech you seem to have, what's to prevent you too from making speeches in the square or in the town hall, like the others of your class? What possesses you, may I ask, to stay in a poor donkey's stable talking to a few ignorant labourers?

AGOSTINO (*to* MATTEO, *who is near the little window*) Keep a look-out, Matteo, if you don't mind; call if you see anything.

MATTEO (*feigning astonishment and leaving the others in suspense for a number of seconds*) Oh, I see several rather shady-looking, in fact very shady-looking . . . trees.

SPINA (*to* AGOSTINO *and* DONATO) You don't know me very well if you think I could change my mind because of anything you said. Once you have overcome the cowardly arguments of egoism and of tacit resignation in yourself, you are not much inclined to respect them in others.

DONATO (*sardonically*) All the same, you can't force us to carry your traps for you on your wild-goose chases.

SPINA No; the struggle will be begun by others, without you, as it's going to be a struggle for everybody's good and everybody's truth, including yours, it will end by attracting and convincing you too and sweeping you into it along with the rest. (*Pause*) In a little while – I hope you don't mind, Agostino – I'm expecting some friends here. I've sent for them from Rome and elsewhere. Maybe they'll settle down in this district. They are going to print a newspaper which will tell the plain truth about the present state of the country and about the new war in Africa. I advise you too to read that truth and to think it over. Together with it, the need for freedom will enter into your souls, and they will come to hunger for it just as the body hungers for food.

DONATO The truth? But every one of us knows the truth already.

SPINA You know the truth already? But which truth is it you're talking about?

DONATO There isn't any truth but one. Poor folks have a bad time of it, that's the truth. How old did you say the world was? Six thousand years? Well, for six thousand years we poor folks have been having a bad time of it, that's the truth.

AGOSTINO Everyone knows that. Such an old truth. To learn a truth like that, there's no need to wear your eyes out over a piece of paper.

MATTEO Poor folks would be a lot better off if instead of being given a piece of paper with such sad and rancid truth on it, they each get a piece of paper with a sausage wrapped up in it.

SCENE 3

The ABOVE, *and* BROTHER GIOACCHINO

> (*The big door in the back wall has opened
> noiselessly. A mendicant* FRIAR, *with an almost
> empty sack over one shoulder, comes into the
> stable after shutting the door behind him; like
> all Capuchin friars he has a beard and tonsure
> and wears a shabby brown habit, held by a
> cincture around his hips; for the rest his appear-
> ance is that of an old and perhaps slightly
> exalted peasant. The* FRIAR *observes the others,
> who are embarrassed and astonished, and fixes
> his gaze on* SPINA, *smiling at him.* SPINA
> *remains impassive*)

AGOSTINO (*to the* FRIAR) Who are you? What are
you doing in my stable?

MATTEO (*to the* FRIAR) Where did you come from?
I didn't see you coming up the path.

DONATO (*recognizing him*) It's brother Gioacchino,
a mendicant friar. (*To the newcomer*) Brother, we're
not bigots, you've come to the wrong door, you've got
no business here.

MATTEO Brother, we're not church mice, we like
the smell of tobacco better than the smell of candles.

BROTHER GIOACCHINO (*confidential and friendly*)
Weren't you talking about truth just now?

AGOSTINO (*stupefied*) We were talking in a whisper;
we were talking about our own affairs; you can't have
understood what we were saying.

BROTHER GIOACCHINO (*nodding assent*) You're right.
We are living in times when truth is a thing to be
spoken about only in whispers and among trusted
friends. (*To* DONATO, *nodding assent*) The poor have a
bad time of it. For six thousand years, as long as the

23

earth has been in existence, they have been having a
bad time. They're downtrodden, humiliated, exploited,
cheated, that is the truth. (*To* SPINA, *in a slower and
softer voice*) And underneath this truth, there is
another less discernible because more profound, but
sister to it, bound up with it and inseparable from it:
the Son of Man is in agony. The crucified Righteous
Man is not dead, as they say; neither has He risen
again and ascended into heaven, as they say; He is
still and for ever in agony on the cross. Nailed hands
and feet to the tree of torment, His side pierced deep
by a lance, His head crowned with sharpest thorns,
spat upon, mocked and abused by the rabble of armed
hirelings, forsaken, betrayed, forgotten by His dearest
friends. He, the Righteous Man, is still on the cross
to-day, hanging between life and death, in atrocious,
unending, fearful, maddening agony. The world
knows nothing of Him, and the Church, maybe out
of pity for us, tries to make us believe that He is
dead and risen again and departed from this earth;
but He is still down here, alive, on the cross, in agony.
That is the truth.

AGOSTINO (*diffident*) Brother, is this just a way
you've got of talking, or . . .

BROTHER GIOACCHINO (*in a low voice*) It is the truth.

DONATO Brother, have you been to the Holy Land?
Did you see Him on Calvary with your own eyes?

MATTEO Brother, did you touch Him with your
hands?

BROTHER GIOACCHINO (*closing his eyes*) I see Him.

MATTEO (*opening his eyes wide*) I don't see Him.

(*In the meantime* SPINA *has withdrawn into a
corner and is feeding the donkey with straw*)

BROTHER GIOACCHINO (*his eyes still closed*) You can
see Him only if you love Him. There's no need to go

24

to Palestine. He is in agony now in this very land. In no country and in no age, perhaps, has the Son of Man been so derided, maltreated, tortured as in this age of ours, in this land of ours. You can discover Him, I tell you, only if you love Him. (*He reopens his eyes and goes out by the little door in the left-hand wall, murmuring:*) The Church tries to console us and to distract our thoughts, making us believe that He is dead and risen again and ascended in triumph to heaven, but He is still down here, in agony. Horrible, appalling, never-ending agony.

AGOSTINO (*calling to* BROTHER GIOACCHINO, *through the little door, which is still open*) Brother, mind the ditch.

> (*In closing the door,* AGOSTINO *is puzzled by something he notices in the distance. He signs to* SPINA *to hurry back to the hayloft, and beckons* DONATO *to approach.* SPINA *remains half-way up the ladder, listening*)

AGOSTINO Who can it be?

DONATO (*watching through the little window*) He doesn't look like a mushroom gatherer.

MATTEO (*also watching*) More likely he's after poisonous mushrooms, I'd say.

DONATO Now he's moving off.

AGOSTINO Now he's coming back again.

MATTEO (*to* DONATO) It's time we were getting along.

DONATO I've stayed longer than I wanted to.

> (DONATO *and* MATTEO *leave by the side door,* SPINA *disappears through the trap-door*)

AGOSTINO, DR. NUNZIO SACCA, PIETRO SPINA

> (AGOSTINO *tidies up some ropes and moves a vat into place. Steps are heard outside the stable and then knocks on the door, which is flung wide before* AGOSTINO *has time to open it, and* DR. NUNZIO SACCA *appears. Although of the same age as Pietro Spina he seems younger; he is dressed correctly and with taste, in the style of a young country doctor, and carries the customary bag*)

DR. SACCA (*visibly annoyed by the distance he has had to cover*) Is the patient here? It seems I'm now expected to go the round of the stables like a vet.

AGOSTINO (*surprised*) Good morning, doctor. Who are you looking for?

DR. SACCA Your wife came to me, Agostino, she wept, she begged and implored me to come here and help someone who is seriously ill, if I've understood her rightly, a stranger, she said, a very sad case, a casual wayfarer who arrived here last night, or something of the sort.

AGOSTINO (*bewildered*) My wife?

DR. SACCA She cried and stammered and wailed in such a confused way that I didn't understand much of what she said, except that I was to come here at once, in fact to run.

AGOSTINO (*as before*) My wife? Without asking me?

> (SPINA, *unobserved has witnessed the entire scene from the trap-door in the ceiling; after a little hesitation he comes rapidly down the ladder and goes over towards the doctor*)

SPINA (*smiling*) Nunzio, it's you? Agostino, please leave us to ourselves.

(*While* AGOSTINO *goes reluctantly out through the side door,* DR. SACCA *inspects from head to foot the person who has just come down from the hayloft, considerably annoyed by his familiarity of greeting and by the fact that he persists in smiling at him. Suddenly he recognizes* SPINA)

DR. SACCA (*glancing around him, bewildered and terrified*) Pietro Spina? What are you doing here? Have you gone mad?

SPINA (*laughing loudly*) Don't be afraid, come here, sit down. (*He moves the two pack-saddles over between them*) How are you getting on? Wife and children, I suppose, success in your profession, and all the rest of it. Congratulations (*ironically*) Are you a commendatore yet? No? For all your zealous cringing to the powers that be?

DR. SACCA (*pulls himself together, but doesn't succeed in hiding his agitation*) I don't need to sit down. Why should I sit down? Maybe you think I want to get myself compromised by you, to argue with you, to listen to your crazy ideas?

SPINA (*motioning to him to calm down*) I know. I know you have always been a scared rabbit. (*Showing him the door*) You may go. If they haven't yet made you a commendatore, and you're certainly burning to be one, I can suggest an infallible means: run and denounce me to the police.

. DR. SACCA (*pocketing the insult*) I came here because Agostino's wife told me there was someone ill here, seriously ill. (*A pause; he sits down*) Do you feel feverish? Do you have shivering fits?

SPINA (*contemptuously*) I assure you I am in a better way than you are.

DR. SACCA (*as if seized by sudden compassion*)

27

Weren't you safe abroad? Why have you come back to put your head right in the lion's mouth? If you love freedom so much, why didn't you stay in the countries where freedom exists?

SPINA I came back to get a breath of air. (*He goes through the movements of taking a deep breath*)

DR. SACCA The greatest revolutionaries, your masters, who spent long years conspiring for their ideas and overthrew tyrants – they passed their whole lives in exile, so why can't you?

SPINA Perhaps you're right, but I'm not the man to save myself for a great political role later on. I am a very bad revolutionary. Whatever I do, I shan't go back into exile. It's the same with me as with the wines of our part of the country: they don't travel well. Other wines on the contrary seem to be specially made for export.

DR. SACCA And what if they get you?

SPINA Well, of course, prison life is not a bed of roses, but neither is the prospect of it so terrifying as to keep me away from my country. I'm anything but a nationalist, and yet when I'm abroad I feel like a fish out of water. I have had enough of exile. Here I am, and here I stay.

DR. SACCA In that case it's none of my business and I wash my hands of it.

SPINA (*ironically*) I'm glad to hear you quote Scripture; you seem to have preserved some relics of the religious education we received together.

DR. SACCA There's certainly more of it left in you: your fanaticism. You no longer believe in God, but in the peasants; in the same all-or-nothing way, though, as when you believed in God.

(SPINA *makes a gesture as if to say: don't talk about things you don't understand*)

DR. SACCA (*with a sudden inspiration*) Will you let me send word to your grandmother that you're in the neighbourhood?

SPINA (*without taking up the suggestion, sits down beside* DR. SACCA *and seems rapt in a faraway vision*) Yesterday evening, to dodge the police, I came on foot all along the path half-way up the Mountain of the Cross. In the distance I saw the school in which we lived together for almost eight years. Maybe the flower beds we tended are in the garden still. Do you remember my geraniums? On the second floor I suppose there's still the big dormitory, where our beds stood next to each other, so close together that we could talk for hours on end without the prefect noticing it. Do you remember the fantastic plans we made? Do you remember the lessons and discussions with Don Benedetto?

DR. SACCA To me it seems as though you were recalling some prehistoric time; the Stone Age, almost.

SPINA When we left that fantastic world, we found a society such as we had never dreamed of. Each of us had to make his choice: either cut loose or submit. How many years have passed since then? Barely fifteen years, and if anyone were to see us here now, he'd find it hard to believe that until we were eighteen our paths ran parallel and we cherished the same dreams for the future.

DR. SACCA That's true, we belong to two different parties now.

SPINA It might be more correct to say, to two different humanities, or rather, to two different races, if the Germans had not compromised the word. I'm expressing myself in this fashion because, although I'm practically in your hands at the moment, it simply isn't in me to make any pretence of respect for you or anyone else that has behaved as you've done.

DR. SACCA There are a lot of other things that aren't in you either. For instance, to understand that the average man doesn't make any choice at all. The terms of his existence are imposed on him without his opinion being asked. If they happen to be at odds with his own preferences, he waits for them to change.

SPINA And what if they don't change? Does it never occur to you that we only live once?

DR. SACCA (*in a troubled voice*) Yes, it does sometimes. And then I have the definite impression that my real life, the only life that Fate has granted me to live, hasn't yet begun. My present life, with all the renunciations, the humiliations, the time-serving, the vulgarities that fill it from morning till night, seems to me something provisional. My real life has yet to begin, I keep telling myself; no, it can't possibly be this one.

SPINA And that's how your whole life will pass.

DR. SACCA Waiting and hoping for a chance to live.

SPINA You mustn't wait. In exile we spend our lives in waiting too. You must live. You must say: my life, my real and only life, has already begun, and nothing unworthy shall have a part in it.

DR. SACCA But you're raving; what if there is no freedom?

SPINA Freedom is not a thing you can receive as a gift. You can live under a dictatorship and be free, provided you struggle against the dictatorship. Even under a dictatorship, the man who thinks with his own head is a free man. The man who takes up a stand for something he believes to be right is a free man. On the other hand, I know the democracies, and you can take it from me that you can live in the most liberal state on earth, but if you are inwardly slothful, callous, servile, compliant, you are not free at all; despite the absence of any violent coercion, you are a slave. No, you mustn't beg your freedom from others. You have got to take freedom for yourself.

DR. SACCA (*with sincere envy*) You've got the damnedest luck to be as mad as you are.

> (*The increasing roar of a lorry makes* DR. SACCA *jump to his feet*)

SPINA (*smiling*) Don't be afraid. (*The noise of the lorry grows fainter.* SPINA *consults his watch and looks out of the little window*)

SPINA I'm expecting friends.

DR. SACCA I'm going. I'm not in the least curious to make their acquaintance. But as a doctor I'd like, for your health's sake at least . . .

SPINA Come, I'll go part of the way with you through the wood.

DR. SACCA (*surprised*) You know the wood?

SPINA (*smiling*) We came here once with the school, at Whitsun, don't you remember?

DR. SACCA Ah, in prehistoric times. (*As before*) What a memory you have.

> (*The two men go out by the door at the back*)

SCENE 5

ANNINA, ROMEO, MURICA

> (ROMEO, LUIGI MURICA *and* ANNINA *enter, one after the other by the door at the back.* ROMEO *is a factory-worker in his thirties, plainly dressed; he wears a dark pull-over and a beret.* LUIGI MURICA *is somewhat clumsy in appearance, a cross between a poor student and a young peasant; he is about twenty.* ANNINA,

31

his fiancée, looks about the same age; she is of pleasing appearance, a dressmaker by trade, self-possessed, frank and modest in manner; she wears a dark grey dress, simple but in good taste, with long sleeves, a white collar, and a green bow at the throat; her black hair is gathered into two plaits twined around her head)

ANNINA (*stands for a moment in the doorway looking out into the distance*) Where's Pietro going? Who's that with him?

ROMEO He saw us coming; he'll be back.

MURICA (*angrily*) Annina, shut the door.

(ANNINA *shuts it hastily. As soon as she gets inside, she discovers the donkey*)

ANNINA Oh, Luigi, a donkey! Look, a real donkey!

(*She begins to stroke it*)

ROMEO Look out, he bites.

ANNINA (*alluding to the donkey, jokingly*) Is he coming to our meeting too?

MURICA Why shouldn't he, if you do?

ANNINA (*laughing*) You're right this time.

MURICA That's what donkeys always say.

ANNINA (*gravely*) Right again.

(MURICA *looks out of the little window, fuming with irritation*)

ANNINA (*stroking the donkey*) Romeo, come and see what lovely eyes the donkey has got.

ROMEO (*nodding towards* MURICA) You're forgetting, Annina, that you are already engaged to be married and that consequently you've got no right to flirt with other donkeys.

ANNINA (*looking more closely*) They're beautiful, but sad.

ROMEO Most likely he's sad because he can't be a horse.

ANNINA Romeo, don't you think the donkey is looking at me rather queerly?

ROMEO I suppose he has fallen in love with you already. Ah, these Southerners. The moment they set eyes on a woman . . .

MURICA (*out of patience*) I'm going.

ANNINA (*pleadingly*) Patience, Luigi, we've barely arrived.

MURICA (*still irritated*) I haven't got time to waste.

ANNINA (*meekly and politely*) But since you've got nothing to do?

MURICA (*doggedly*) Just for that very reason.

ROMEO (*making an effort to control himself*) I don't understand you, Murica. You're becoming a riddle to me.

ANNINA (*interrupting him*) Now, Romeo, please don't start off again in the tone of yesterday evening. Forgive me, Romeo, I'm only a dressmaker and I'd hold my tongue if it were a question of theories, but when it comes to personal matters I've got a right to have my say, and I take the liberty of saying that there should be real brotherhood between comrades and that we should all love each other and treat each other with respect even when one of us happens to be tired or a bit irritable.

ROMEO (*conciliatory*) Annina, you know as well as I do that there has never been the slightest conflict of ideas nor personal friction between Murica and us. We've all admired him since the day he left the university in order to learn printing at top speed and devote himself to working for the illegal press. It doesn't happen every day that a comrade gives up his career to serve the revolutionary cause, and every one

C

of us is grateful to him for this immense sacrifice. But now, just when we've set up our little printing press in accordance with his own instructions, I can't for the life of me understand why every day he thinks up a new pretext for not bringing out the newspaper. Annina, do you know why? Can you explain it to me?

MURICA (*venomously*) If you want information about me, Romeo, you don't need, you really don't need to ask others for it in my presence.

ANNINA (*imploring* ROMEO *with a glance not to answer* MURICA, *not to follow up the altercation*) Luigi's nerves are a bit frayed, Romeo, that's the truth of the matter. Maybe he could do with a little rest. Couldn't the printing of the paper be postponed for a few days? It's a passing tiredness. Luigi's nerves have been a bit worn ever since the last time he was arrested.

MURICA (*in a tone of distaste*) Annina, your kindness is both superfluous and exasperating.

ANNINA (*resigned and polite*) I'm so sorry, Luigi; of course you're right, no man wants pity from a woman; you know, I can understand your feelings perfectly; I'm stupid, but not as stupid as all that. Besides, our life is getting to be more difficult every day – I'm not talking about you now, Luigi, but in general, about all of us – and it's not surprising if our nerves get frayed. That's why we've got to be kind to each other; patient and considerate.

> (MURICA *looks out of the little window and the dialogue continues between* ANNINA *and* ROMEO *as though he were not present*)

ROMEO A true revolutionary, Annina, mustn't have these so-called 'nerves'. You're right, Annina, our life is very hard and dangerous; and if we can't manage to keep our nerves out of the game, we shall end up in a madhouse.

ANNINA Do you think it possible to live without nerves, Romeo?

ROMEO In a revolution, the only combatants who are of any use, the only ones who survive, are those who manage to keep their nerves out of the game.

ANNINA How is it done, Romeo?

ROMEO It's difficult. It's a sort of narcosis.

ANNINA But, Romeo – forgive me for asking stupid questions: how can we possibly be true and courageous fighters for the revolution if we have been put to sleep? Are we going to turn into a movement of sleep-walkers?

ROMEO The enemy thinks he can terrorize us, so we must manage to put our normal sensibility to sleep, we must chloroform it; otherwise I tell you we'll go mad, Annina.

ANNINA And what if it is just because of our sensibility that we have come to the revolutionary cause? What if we are there just because our sensibility was wounded by the pitilessness, the injustice, the ugliness of human society as it is now? By annihilating our sensibility, Romeo, wouldn't we be destroying in ourselves the very feelings that led us to the revolution?

ROMEO It's possible, Annina, and sometimes it does happen as you say. Men are sometimes turned away from our movement by the same feelings which originally led them into it. Annina: never trust sentimental revolutionaries.

ANNINA You're undoubtedly going to be disappointed in me, and with good reason, but I don't want to deceive you or to deceive our comrades. I must confess to you that I couldn't conceive of my life without any feelings in it.

ROMEO What I mean is this: we must merge our

normal feelings in our will to fight. We must draw them away from our skin and our nerves and hide them in our bones.

ANNINA And in that way you think we become insensible to pain, Romeo? Romeo, do you think Spina has put his nerves out of the game?

(*The door at the back opens and* PIETRO SPINA *enters*)

SCENE 6

The ABOVE, *and* PIETRO SPINA

SPINA (*leaving the door ajar behind him*) Cicala will be here in a few minutes; I saw him in his cart coming along the valley. Sorry I'm late; I needed to stretch my legs, so I walked through the wood with Dr. Sacca, an old school friend of mine.

MURICA (*in astonishment*) The doctor? Don't you know how compromised he is? Don't you know what brutal injustices he has countenanced?

SPINA I know. And I pity him.

ANNINA (*whispers to* ROMEO *who is standing near her*) Pity? Did he say pity?

SPINA (*to* ROMEO) Have you news of your wife?

ROMEO No.

SPINA Has she been taken to a clinic?

ROMEO Possibly.

SPINA So maybe you're already a father without knowing it?

ROMEO (*feigning indifference*) Maybe.

SPINA Couldn't we send Annina to find out?

ANNINA (*eagerly*) Oh, of course, Romeo, you know how glad I'd be.

36

ROMEO (*annoyed*) The house is watched.

SPINA But if she's in the clinic . . .

ROMEO The police will be expecting me to visit my wife, and they'll have her watched at the clinic too. Besides, Annina has other things to do.

ANNINA I could go and find out from the doctor at his home.

ROMEO (*to* SPINA) The first condition we lay down for comrades who accept the clandestine way of life is a complete break with family ties. You respect this condition; why shouldn't I?

SPINA (*to* ANNINA) We'll have a talk about this another time.

ROMEO (*to* SPINA) I've been to Luco and Trasacco, and I've been to see the people you told me about. They're poor old men who haven't budged an inch since before the Flood. Nothing doing.

SPINA With Agostino and Donato, here, I haven't had any better results. There is something still worse than to be forcibly deprived of freedom, and that is, either to be completely lacking in the need for freedom, or to have it atrophied. It's hard to ride the Flood backwards, to ride back against the current to the times before the Flood. And yet, Romeo, we have to try.

MURICA (*who has been taking in every word of* SPINA'S *with great interest, repeats with conviction*) 'Either to be completely lacking in the need for freedom or to have it atrophied.' Perhaps you were thinking of that too, Spina, when in your warning to the Italians that you sent me yesterday to set up in type, you wrote this sentence: 'The person who becomes aware of his humanity.' Since yesterday I've never stopped thinking about that sentence. You know when you set by hand, slowly, letter by letter, you read the words in a different way. Sometimes the compositor doesn't

37

bother about the meaning; in fact it's well-known that the best compositors are those who don't think about the meaning of the copy or don't understand it, and see only the letters. But I'm not a real compositor, and it often happens, when I'm composing the words by hand, letter by letter, that I feel them with an intensity I'd never known before, and I discover the inner charge, so to speak, of every word, its hidden explosive force. Well, ever since yesterday I've been wrestling with this phrase of yours: 'The person who becomes aware of his humanity'; that is to say, the person who has been driven by some particular anguish of his own to search for the inmost sense of human life, and eventually finds it and absorbs it into his awareness. I'd like to ask you some questions about this point but I quite understand that you haven't got time now.

(ROMEO *keeps looking out of the little window while* SPINA *and* ANNINA *are listening to* MURICA; SPINA *with deep attention, the girl with increasing anxiety and emotion*)

ROMEO (*crossing to the door at the back*) Here's Cicala coming.

SPINA (*to* MURICA) Thanks, Murica, for taking my words so seriously; although, to be frank, it almost makes me afraid. It's a warning to me to weigh every word I write in future.

(*In the meantime the door at the back has opened wide and* CICALA *the knife grinder has appeared with his cart in the doorway*)

We ought to see more of each other, Murica, and get to know each other better.

(ANNINA *goes over to* MURICA *and puts her arm through his very tenderly*)

SCENE 7

The ABOVE, *and* CICALA; *then* ANNINA *and* SPINA *alone*
(CICALA *has the appearance of an ordinary itinerant knife grinder. He leaves his cart outside the door and comes inside to hand* SPINA *a package which the latter places in the manger*)

CICALA (*to* SPINA) They've given the alarm about you all over the place. Last night the police were looking for you at your uncle Don Bastiano's and at your grandmother Donna Maria Vincenza's.

SPINA (*to* CICALA) Thanks. Annina will let you know to-night where to find me in future. (*To the others*) You'd better disappear gradually too.

(CICALA, ROMEO, MURICA *leave at short intervals one by one, the first two by the door at the back,* MURICA *by the side door.* ANNINA, *on the point of following* MURICA, *turns back to* SPINA *who is busy opening the package he had placed in the manger*)

ANNINA (*with emotion in her voice*) Pietro, I beg of you, be prudent. I'm only a simple comrade and I've no right to give you advice; but my opinion as a simple comrade is that each of us should be the other's keeper, each of us is responsible for the other.

SPINA (*smiling*) How long have you been in our movement?

ANNINA Two years. Don't you remember it was you that converted me?

SPINA And how do you feel in it?

ANNINA Good. When I was a schoolgirl, please don't laugh, I used to dream of becoming a nun. (*She blushes*) Not to live in a convent and only with women, as you can imagine, but to go and nurse lepers. Now I feel . . .

39

SPINA (*pretending to be offended*) Ah, so you consider me a leper?

ANNINA (*silencing him and continuing in a slow voice, like someone confessing a secret*) Now I feel as though I had entered the novitiate of a way of life that is pure and consecrated to duty, a way of life that in its own way is also sacred, because in its own way it's difficult, and farther removed than any other from the compromises of ordinary life. But now you are certainly laughing at me.

SPINA (*somewhat moved*) Yes, an outlaw's life can be a great thing, Annina, a great good fortune, a great freedom, a daily dialogue on the things that really matter. An outlaw's life can also be a means of not growing old, of continuing to dream of always staying young. (*Jokingly*) If you shut your eyes, for instance, how old would you take me to be?

ANNINA (*shutting her eyes*) Eighteen. And how old would you think me, if you shut your eyes?

SPINA With my eyes shut or open, sixteen.

(ANNINA *laughs and runs out by the door in centre back*)

CURTAIN

ACT II

*The stage is divided into two parts: two-thirds of it repre-
sents the ground-floor wine-shop of a provincial inn.
The remaining third, on a somewhat higher level and to
the audience's right, represents the interior of a room in
the same inn. Both rooms – separated by a thin wall and
communicating by a door which is reached by climbing
three steps from the larger room – are visible to the
audience. The door in the back wall of the wine-shop is
also the main entrance to the inn and opens on to a little
square; a green branch hangs, in accordance with local
custom, over the doorway, announcing to passers-by that
wine is sold retail; through the doorway a small table
and a chair can be seen on the pavement. Inside, to the
left near the door, is the bar; on the counter stand wine-
bowls, a demijohn, glasses; behind the counter, fixed to
the wall, a rack with a few shelves of bottles and flasks.
There are two tables and some chairs for customers. An
old-fashioned gramophone, with a horn, stands on one
of the tables. The walls are adorned with a motley
assortment of pictures and inscriptions, such as: a skull
and cross-bones with the legend 'Me ne frego' (I don't
give a damn); 'Sabato trippa' (Tripe on Saturdays);
'Vietato sputare' (Do not spit); 'Volete la salute?
Bevete l'Amaro Sant'Agostino' (Do you want to keep
healthy? Drink Saint Augustine's Bitters). A permanently open door in the left wall leads to the interior
of the inn.*

*The partition occupying the right-hand side of the
stage is the room of Don Paolo Spada, 'a priest from
another diocese', and it contains the bare essentials of a
bedroom: a low divan, a night-table with a bedside lamp,
a holy picture, a table, a chair; in the back wall there is
a window with closed shutters; beside the window a
mirror.*

SCENE 1

The LANDLADY, ULIVA, THREE WORTHIES, DON PAOLO SPADA

(*The* LANDLADY *is an elderly woman, dressed in black, with a wealth of old-fashioned trimmings and lace; her hair is gathered into a large bun at the nape of her neck; she is a commanding, stately figure, not at all obliging. Seated in a corner,* ULIVA *appears to be a casual wayfarer taking a short rest; he is a stranger to the place, a poorly-dressed young man, well-bred, reserved, decorous; the only exceptional thing about him is his striking impassivity; he remains seated, silent and motionless, a glass of water in front of him. The* THREE WORTHIES *belong to the ancient, picturesque and parasitic caste of rural authorities; despite the antiquity of the species, in their personal adornment they follow closely the tailor's dummy of the period; waved and pomaded locks, fancy necktie, exaggeratedly long jacket with pagoda-shaped shoulders and narrow hips, light brown shoes or spats, enormous signet ring on the little finger, they have an air of authoritative buoyant patronage. It is thought superfluous to indicate these personages by name; the* FIRST WORTHY *can be distinguished from the others by his little pointed beard.* DON PAOLO SPADA *is* PIETRO SPINA *disguised as a priest; the soutane, the spectacles and the tonsure modify his appearance considerably; the audience can however still recognize him. Throughout the first scene he remains alone and well in view in the room adjoining the wine-shop. He alternates writing at the table with practising make-up in front of the mirror*)

42

LANDLADY (*ensconced behind the counter; to the* THREE WORTHIES *as they enter by the door at the back*) Have they really got him?

FIRST WORTHY (*crossing to the gramophone and choosing a record*) There was a misunderstanding; it wasn't him after all.

SECOND WORTHY The fellow looked like him, but wasn't him.

THIRD WORTHY He had the same crease in his trousers, the chief of the police said, identically the same; but as for the rest of him — it was somebody else.

LANDLADY Somebody else? They've let him go, then?

FIRST WORTHY Not likely. It wasn't him, but it was, after all, somebody else, so they have to make inquiries in any case, you can see that for yourself.

SECOND WORTHY (*lounging on the table and resting his feet on a chair*) When you come to think of it, if it isn't him, it's more than likely to be somebody else. And besides, the police have their reputation to think of; so you see . . .

LANDLADY (*irate*) Reputation be damned. If the man is innocent, if he was arrested by mistake, why should he stay in gaol?

FIRST WORTHY (*trying a Caruso record on the gramophone and letting it play softly so as not to disturb the conversation*) How can you say he is innocent? Have you forgotten what the Church teaches? No man is wholly and entirely innocent.

LANDLADY (*in amazement*) When did you take to going to church?

THIRD WORTHY (*munching salted roast peanuts, a handful of which he has dexterously removed from a plate on the counter*) A couple of weeks ago. Because of the schoolgirls in the confirmation class.

SECOND WORTHY Some are really sweet little things.

43

FIRST WORTHY (*changing the record and mimicking the tone of a preacher*) No man is wholly and entirely innocent, the parish priest explained last Sunday. If not awake at least in dreams, he said, every man some time or other covets his neighbour's house or his neighbour's cow or his neighbour's wife. If not awake, at least in dreams. Consequently, even if an innocent man gets arrested by mistake, in actual fact he is not really innocent and therefore his arrest is never a mistake. And if he is kept awhile in gaol, he is merely getting what he deserves in any case, and maybe only a part of what he deserves. Amen.

SECOND WORTHY (*to* ULIVA, *whom he does not know*) Would you care to have the honour of playing billiards with us? Yes? Well then, first and foremost you might buy us a drink.

> (ULIVA *does not reply nor even look at his inter-locutor; he keeps an eye on the door of* DON PAOLO'S *room, waiting for it to open, and shows no sign of following the conversation between the* LANDLADY *and the* WORTHIES)

LANDLADY (*to the* FIRST WORTHY, *after some reflection*) Does what you said a little while ago apply to everybody?

FIRST WORTHY Everybody.

LANDLADY Even the powers that be?

> (*Caruso's song on the gramophone comes to an abrupt stop*)

FIRST WORTHY ⎱
SECOND WORTHY ⎰ Eh? What's that? In heaven's name, what are you thinking of?
THIRD WORTHY

LANDLADY (*imperturbably*) I suppose the powers that be aren't men?

FIRST WORTHY Yes, of course, they're men, but exceptional men.

44

SECOND WORTHY Men who make the laws themselves.

THIRD WORTHY And for themselves they have made
a special law.

LANDLADY And so that's why they can never be
caught? And so that's why they're exceptional? Ah,
now I understand why the powers that be can't lay
their hands on Pietro Spina. He too, in his own way,
has made himself a special law.

> (*In the adjoining room* DON PAOLO *is now intent
> on counting the buttons of his soutane, from
> collar to feet and back again; next he counts the
> wrist buttons; the calculation is laborious*)

FIRST WORTHY A special law?

LANDLADY He too, in his own way, is a law unto
himself.

SECOND WORTHY And he's made a special law for
himself, has he? But he's got no right to make laws as
the fancy takes him.

LANDLADY He has made himself a special law.
Haven't you heard of it? He has taken for himself the
right to do it. He has made himself a new standard of
right and wrong. And the things the authorities find
right he finds wrong, and the things the authorities
find wrong he finds right, and the things the authorities make much of he despises, and the things the
authorities detest he loves, and the things we all set
so much store by he pays no heed to, and the things
that none of us pay any heed to he venerates. Ah, I
know his kind. Believe me, it's not easy to hold
them captive.

THIRD WORTHY So he really is a madman, you say.

LANDLADY You can kill him, but you cannot hold
him captive. I don't know how to explain it; I tell
you what it is, he is beyond your reach. He belongs

to another world. I have never seen Pietro Spina, but I know the breed An ancient breed it is.

FIRST WORTHY It is a breed of madmen that will be uprooted and destroyed.

LANDLADY A proud breed it is, I tell you, that has far-reaching and stubborn roots. It has made itself a standard of wrong and of right that is different from the usual one. As soon as you root it out in one place it springs up again in another. I know the breed. Ah, it's not easy to take it prisoner.

SECOND WORTHY The man that wedded you and then left you alone with the children and went off to die of despair in Brazil, was he too of that accursed breed?

LANDLADY (*furious, then touched by the memory*) If he detested the things that you set store by and loved those that you detest, how was he to go on living here? In his own way, he had made himself a special law, different from yours, the very opposite of yours, and he had to go away. And yet, far from his country he couldn't live for long. His gentle spirit had left its tenderest roots behind. And without the bread and the wine and the oil of these parts, without this air, without these stones, without his woman, how could he live for long?

FIRST WORTHY You say he lived according to a special law? What kind of law was it?

(*In the doorway at the back there appears* DON ZABAGLIONE)

LANDLADY A proud breed it is, and headstrong, a truly unaccommodating breed. I know it. Ah, it's not easy to hold it captive.

SECOND WORTHY And for the sake of that crazy idea of his, he left you to live alone? At that time I suppose you were still young.

Scene 2

The ABOVE, *and* DON ZABAGLIONE

The lawyer MARCO TUGLIO-ZABAGLIA, *also known as* DON
ZABAGLIONE, *is a rubicund, portly, gouty and yet
handsome play-actor. Once a popular idol, he has preserved from those bygone times only the custom of the
wide-brimmed hat, having reconciled it in an artistic
fashion with the little pointed beard, Balbo style, which
he loyally adopted together with the new ideas. Also
worthy of mention is the walking-stick which emphasizes
his every gesture.*

> (DON ZABAGLIONE *greets from the threshold both
> the present and the absent with a sweeping
> flourish of his hat, and then turns to the* THREE
> WORTHIES)

DON ZABAGLIONE Bright hopes of our Mother
Country, how goes your appetite?
FIRST WORTHY Heroically.
SECOND WORTHY And your digestion, indefatigable
seducer of the populace?
DON ZAGABLIONE With iron discipline, I thank you.
(*To the* THREE WORTHIES, *pointing in the direction of
the square*) Out there they are anxiously awaiting you
for the meeting, Let me exhort you to concord. This
is a historic day and all factious spirits must hold their
peace.

> (*The* THREE WORTHIES *go out*)

LANDLADY (*to* DON ZABAGLIONE) When **are** you
going to make your speech?
DON ZABAGLIONE As soon as the dignitaries come
to an agreement about a few liturgical details.

47

(*Complacently*) The arcade and the courtyard of the town hall are already swarming with an impatient multitude.

LANDLADY I'll run and put out the flags.

DON ZABAGLIONE (*pointing to* DON PAOLO'S *room*) Is the crow in his nest?

LANDLADY (*nodding*) He's praying. He prays all day long.

> (*She goes out by the door in the left wall*)
> (*In front of the mirror* DON PAOLO *is trying on a pair of dark glasses, but perhaps he finds his double in the mirror rather melancholy and ridiculous, because he sticks out his tongue at him*)

DON ZABAGLIONE *to* ULIVA (*whom he does not know*) Young gentleman, young stranger, I do not doubt it was in order to hear my historic speech that you came to this obscure parish. Are you a chronicler of some gazette? Do you desire an impressive interview?

> (ULIVA *looks at him indifferently, without answering*. DON ZABAGLIONE *knocks with his stick at the door of* DON PAOLO'S *room. The latter hurriedly puts out of sight some papers lying on the table and opens the door*)

SCENE 3

DON ZABAGLIONE, DON PAOLO, ULIVA

DON ZABAGLIONE (*bowing*) Your reverence, I devoutly kiss your consecrated hands. Have I perhaps disturbed you in your prayers?

DON PAOLO (*shutting the door of his room behind him and coming down the three steps*) I was expecting you. I should like to continue yesterday evening's conversation.

(DON PAOLO, *noticing* ULIVA'S *presence, greets him behind* DON ZABAGLIONE'S *back and signs to him to wait*)

DON ZABAGLIONE Our providential meeting of yesterday evening was a delicious appetiser for my weary old soul, your reverence. At dinner my wife was dumbfounded by my appetite. I've met a saint, I had to explain to her, a real saint.

DON PAOLO (*with a protective allusion*) I shall mention you to His Grace.

(*Impelled by an irresistible surge of fellow-feeling* DON ZABAGLIONE *suddenly embraces him and kisses him on both cheeks.* DON PAOLO *has to dry his face*)

DON ZABAGLIONE (*deeply moved*) I thank you. Not for myself, but for the people's sake, I thank you. A felicitous harmony between sacred and profane oratory has always been the surest foundation for the prosperity of kingdoms.

DON PAOLO (*in adulatory tones*) I can't understand why an orator of your ability has remained secluded in such an obscure part of the world.

DON ZABAGLIONE Ah yes, my wings are too big for my nest. 'Maiores pennas nido.' Everything is small here, everything is petty, low, dwarfish. Except envy. (*Bitterly, in a whisper*) The envy here is gigantic.

DON PAOLO Do they reproach you with political inconsistency? There was a time, if I'm not mistaken, when you were a Socialist?

DON ZABAGLIONE (*contemptuously*) Consistency is the virtue of the inarticulate. You must admit it would be idiotic for a true orator to keep repeating the same words all his life.

DON PAOLO For the sake of certain words, which you

too helped to spread, many simple persons, many inarticulate persons, if you like to put it that way, have faced grave sacrifices.

DON ZABAGLIONE Sacrifice, ah, what a beautiful word it is. Sacrifice, you know, is what I most admire in Christianity. What compromised Marxism, you as a priest must allow that I am right, was its materialism. I'm quite aware that there are Socialists, as you have recalled just now, who have sacrificed their daily bread, their career, their comforts, for their idea. But what does all that amount to compared to my sacrifice? I have sacrificed something far loftier and far more precious: the Idea itself. A spiritual sacrifice, whatever Marxism may have to say about it, is worth far more than a material sacrifice. But who can appreciate the meaning of spiritual sacrifice better than a priest?

DON PAOLO You are a hero.

DON ZABAGLIONE I thank you. And allow me to add: an unrecognized hero. After a dozen years of sincere and total adherence to the new eloquence, to-day I am still held in suspicion. What has made me suffer most of all in these last years has been having to hold my tongue when there were so many golden opportunities that cried to heaven for an orator, for someone to sweep the populace off its feet and raise it to the dizzy summits of history. In this way important events have gone completely to waste, and that, if you come to think of it, is the most tragic thing that could happen. To-day, for the first time, I am once again being allowed to speak at a public ceremony.

DON PAOLO Is it a meeting for the war in Africa? What you are going to speak about?

DON ZABAGLIONE A magnificent subject: the Roman tradition in this region. I hope you will honour me with your presence.

DON PAOLO You think there exists a genuine Roman tradition in this part of the country?

DON ZABAGLIONE (*confidentially*) Your reverence, what's this you're asking me? You don't take me for an illiterate, now do you? Strictly between ourselves, the so-called Roman tradition, historically speaking, is sheer humbug. In our part of the country and throughout Southern Italy, which is just where the Roman tradition ought to be strongest, there isn't a trace of it to be found. Our only tradition is Bourbon, Spanish, possibly Christian. Just talk to our old people, your reverence. You'll hear nothing from them but tales of disasters, famines, cholera epidemics, hangings, witches, saints and miracles. Rome is merely a goal for pilgrimages. Besides, you are aware that there was no Roman influence here even in Roman times. The religion, the language, the alphabet, the customs, the race of the peoples of this region were altogether different from those of Latium. But as a theme for eloquence your reverence cannot deny that the Roman tradition is a perfect gold-mine. Well, I don't want to anticipate now, you'll be hearing me shortly.

> (*From the square comes the confused shouting of two groups of people in grave dispute: two words, almost two opposed battle-cries, seem to prevail over the others: pig and calf. The hubbub approaches the inn*)

SCENE 4

The ABOVE, *the* THREE WORTHIES, VILLAGERS
> (*The* THREE WORTHIES *of a little while ago, followed by other persons who, however, remain standing outside the inn door, reappear in order to explain the cause of the hub-bub to* DON

51

ZABAGLIONE *and to seek his arbitration. The* FIRST *and* THIRD WORTHIES *represent the opposing parties, and they are worked up to such a pitch that the* SECOND WORTHY *has difficulty in keeping them apart; as long as the* THREE WORTHIES *and the persons remaining at the door persist in talking all together, nobody will understand very much beyond the opposing cries of pig and calf. During the entire scene* DON PAOLO *seated beside* ULIVA, *remains silent*)

DON ZABAGLIONE (*calling for silence and obtaining it with sweeping pacificatory gestures*) My friends, before acquainting myself with the profound cause of your dissension, since I know you all and love you all impartially, grant me, I beg you, to voice my conviction that the origin of your impassioned dispute is surely a most noble one and undoubtedly concerns the best way of rendering disinterested service to our beloved country. (*Signs of lively approval*) Nothing but this confidence in your innate idealism could make me hope that despite my demerits I may succeed in reconciling you. (*As above*) Well then, what is it all about?

SECOND WORTHY If the difficult task of expounding the motive of this sudden split in the patriotic ranks now falls to my most unworthy person, it is only because, as between the two parties, my point of view is, so to speak, intermediary. (*Unanimous interruptions from the door:* 'Coward, turncoat, busybody') Well, when we were discussing the bill of fare for the banquet to celebrate the beginning of the new war in Africa, there broke out among us an unbridgeable difference of opinion on the question of principle as to whether veal or pork be the more savoury meat. Two parties, one may say, were immediately formed: the Pig Party and the Calf Party. In vain I endeavoured to argue that both meats have their merits, according to season, according to the state of one's appetite, according to the sauce or condiment . . . (*Interruptions from the door:* 'Coward, turncoat, no compromises') In the face of your fanatical intolerance, there is nothing left for me to do but yield the floor to the direct representatives of the two conflicting parties. Here we have (*Showing* DON ZABAGLIONE *the* FIRST WORTHY) the most ardent supporter of the Calf Party. (*Interruption from some favourers of the Pig*: 'He's that way for family reasons, what can you expect, he's got a wife') Here (*Indicating the* THIRD WORTHY) on the other hand, is the authentic and intransigent leader of the Pig Party. (*Interruptions from some partisans of the Calf:* 'He can't help it, he was born that way, he's got moral reasons').

> (DON ZABAGLIONE *smiles and with a slight friendly gesture of his hand signifies his desire to speak. In a few moments there is dead silence. The bystanders are dazzled and fascinated by his calm serene sovereign smile, a smile bestowed in equal measure on the partisans of the Pig and on those of the Calf, and nevertheless, in its clarity, entirely free from all intent to compromise. He puts his hat down on the table and strokes with a slow, sensuous gesture, his beard and moustache. With polished art he prolongs the pause, still smiling. When he begins to speak, the tender and mellifluous cadence of his voice and the emotion it betrays such as no one can recall having heard for many years*)

DON ZABAGLIONE Your query as to whether pork or veal be more flattering to the palate moves me (this is no idle boast but a sincere confession) to the inmost recesses of my being. And nevertheless, my friends,

if I am to reply truthfully and impartially to the
dilemma which, with grave danger to law and order,
justly impassions and divides us, I needs must bid the
senses be silent. The senses drug the brain. I therefore submit your query to history; I submit it to the
fine arts and to literature; to science and to theology.
I ask the artists to tell me the source of their inspiration and the hermits the cause of their torments; I ask
the man in the street for the key to his dreams. If only
they could reply in a language comprehensible to me,
I should ask the same question of the birds of the air,
the beasts of the jungle, the fishes of the sea; but for
them science can testify, and that suffices for me.
And here, my friends, is the wonderful answer that
reconciles us and fraternally unites us all; here is the
joyful solution of the agonizing, the tragic enigma. In
truth, there exists nothing choicer, more delicious,
more delicate, more exquisite or more piquant on the
face of the earth, than the sweet companion of the
male, the female.

> (*The instant this last word is uttered, an out-
> burst of enthusiasm sweeps away, as though by
> magic, all trace of dissension between the sup-
> porters of the Pig and those of the Calf; the
> WORTHIES kiss and embrace DON ZABAGLIONE;
> the same scene of deepfelt fraternization takes
> place among the persons who have remained in
> the doorway. But suddenly a distant flourish of
> trumpets heralds the beginning of the public
> ceremony, and a few moments later the wine-shop
> is empty of people. DON PAOLO takes ULIVA into
> his room. Through the inn door people can be
> seen marching from left to right in what is pre-
> sumably the direction of the meeting, until from
> outside someone, perhaps one of the inn servants,*

54

*half-shuts the door. During the whole of the
following scene the wine-shop remains empty and
in partial shadow*)

SCENE 5

ULIVA, DON PAOLO, *voice of* DON ZABAGLIONE, *voices of
the* CROWD

DON PAOLO (*anxiously*) Hasn't the knife-grinder
passed yet?

ULIVA No. Just listen to what's happened. The new
printing-press . . .

DON PAOLO Has the paper been printed? Is it ready
for distribution?

ULIVA The new printing-press too was discovered
and seized this morning at dawn.

DON PAOLO (*starting*) Annina, Murica – were they
arrested?

ULIVA They were not there.

DON PAOLO (*stricken*) Seized. The new printing-
press destroyed too.

ULIVA It was Romeo told me; he was in a hurry and
gave no details. He was in a hurry, he had the feeling
he was being shadowed. If they haven't got him,
he may be here shortly and he'll tell you about it
himself.

DON PAOLO (*almost to himself*) So the war will break
out and there won't be a single public protest from us.

ULIVA We can hardly ask them to postpone the war
just because you are not yet able to sabotage it.

DON PAOLO Blindfold like sheep the soldiers will go
to the slaughter.

ULIVA Well, after all, perhaps that's the least painful

55

way of dying. An increase of consciousness, mark my words, always means an increase of suffering. A humanitarian like you should reflect on that.

DON PAOLO It would mean an intensification of pain only if our conscience were by nature condemned exclusively to contemplation and were powerless to change the course of events.

ULIVA (*abandoning for the time his tone of indifference and almost of boredom and expressing himself with lively conviction*) I know what kind of events you think would prove the victory of conscience – revolutions; but if you examine them closely, they prove exactly the opposite. Believe me, my dear boy, exactly the opposite. But I don't advise a good fellow like you to examine them too closely. (DON PAOLO *wants to interrupt, but* ULIVA *cuts him short*) Let me speak. I've got something else to tell you too, namely that the soutane suits you very well; remarkably well in fact; congratulations. Don't you think it would be a good idea to make it obligatory, together with the tonsure, for all officials of the Party?

DON PAOLO (*jokingly*) Celibacy, too?

ULIVA Of course. All the more so since celibacy doesn't exclude the rest, not even polygamy; rather the contrary.

> (*Through the closed bedroom window comes the sound of applause from a crowd gathered for a public meeting.* DON PAOLO *opens the window. The voice of an orator can be heard distinctly, if somewhat attenuated by distance*)

VOICE OF DON ZABAGLIONE Descendants of Rome eternal, O you, my people! Tell me, who was it brought civilization and culture to the Mediterranean and to all that was then known of Africa?

VOICES OF THE CROWD We did!

VOICE OF DON ZABAGLIONE Tell me further, I beg thee, who brought civilization and culture to the whole of Europe, even to the foggy shores of England, and built cities on the very soil where savages, together with wild boars and stags, used to grub for food?

VOICES OF THE CROWD We did!

VOICE OF DON ZABAGLIONE Tell me again, I implore thee, who discovered America?

VOICES OF THE CROWD We did! We did! We did!

VOICE OF DON ZABAGLIONE Tell me yet again, I entreat you, who invented electricity, the radio, and all the conveniences, wonders and beauties of modern life?

VOICES OF THE CROWD We did!

VOICE OF DON ZABAGLIONE And lastly, tell me, if you please, what race was it that went all over the world to dig mines, build bridges, make roads, drain swamps?

VOICES OF THE CROWD We did! We did! We did!

VOICE OF DON ZABAGLIONE Well, now I shall explain to you the origins of our wretchedness. Whatever civilization there is in this world of ours, the best part of it is the work of our hands. But the other nations have robbed us of it. However, after centuries of humiliation and injustice, Divine Providence has at last sent our country the Man who will see to it that we get back everything that belongs to us and that the others have taken from us.

VOICES OF THE CROWD To London! To London!

OTHER VOICES To New York! To Philadelphia!

OTHER VOICES To São Paolo! to the Avenida Paulista! to the Avenida Angelica!

OTHER VOICES To Buenos Aires!

A VOICE To New York! To Forty-Second Street!

OTHER VOICES What is there at Forty-Second Street?

THE VOICE You'll see what there is! Christ be our helper, to Forty-Second Street!

VOICE OF DON ZABAGLIONE First-born heir of immortal Rome, O you, my people . . .

> (DON PAOLO *slams the window to, cutting short the orator's voice*)

DON PAOLO (*angrily*) What a play-actor! What a buffoon!

ULIVA And yet, in ten or fifteen years' time, if as may very well happen there is a shuffle of dictatorships, you will step right into the shoes of Don Zabaglione. What I mean to say is, you will inherit his function as a windbag.

DON PAOLO You know, Uliva, witticisms, if they are to be witty, should contain some wit; otherwise they are vulgar banalities.

ULIVA Of course, there'll be a certain difference. Unlike Don Zabaglione, you'll believe what you say. I have always admired your unlimited capacity for believing.

DON PAOLO And as for your cynicism, I have never taken it seriously. Otherwise I couldn't understand why you should have stayed with us all these years, and why you are with us still. It's certainly not for the sake of convenience.

ULIVA That's where you're wrong; it happens to be just for the sake of convenience. What I mean is, I've stayed with you and your friends because you are persecuted, and in a certain sense that happened to suit me. As you see, for all my cynicism, it's a sentimental reason, almost frivolous in fact. Now however I feel myself ready to part company.

DON PAOLO Are you so convinced that our ideal is to exchange the role of victims for that of persecutors?

ULIVA It's not your ideal, no; but it's undoubtedly your destiny.

58

DON PAOLO Destiny is the **excuse** of weaklings and defeatists.

ULIVA It would be too easy if we could give it the slip just by shutting our eyes to it.

DON PAOLO And I maintain that nothing will ever induce us to sacrifice the essence of our ideal to the success of our ideal.

ULIVA Nothing? If the word destiny isn't to your liking, you can put the word history in its place.

DON PAOLO Our history hasn't yet been written.

ULIVA You haven't yet read it, but it has long been written. Or rather, you have probably read it without ever realizing that it was your own history and that of your friends.

DON PAOLO One can add new pages to history.

ULIVA By copying the old ones, and adding spelling mistakes.

DON PAOLO (*in a tone of distaste*) You know, Uliva, quibbling is no argument.

ULIVA You've always tried to run away from real arguments. I'll give you a real argument now: every revolution, every one of them, without a single exception, began as a movement of freedom and ended up as a tyranny. There was never yet a revolution that escaped that fate.

DON PAOLO That's not true, but even if it were true, we ought to say: the revolutions of the past have turned to ashes, we will make one that will keep its promise.

ULIVA Illusions, illusions. Perhaps we'll have economic changes, thanks to which, just as we now have State railways, State quinine, State salt, State matches, and State tobacco, so in the same way we shall then have State bread, State shoes, State shirts, State underpants, State potatoes, and fresh State peas. Will that be progress, from a technical standpoint? Let's be generous and admit it will. But this technical innovation will fall into the hands of a privileged caste which will profess official shibboleths and will use every means, from the cinema to terrorism, to stamp out all trace of heresy and tyrannize the people. The present inquisition will be succeeded by a Red inquisition. The present censorship by a Red censorship. Instead of the present deportations there will be Red deportations, of which dissident revolutionaries will be the favourite victims. Just as the present bureaucracy identifies itself with patriotism and exterminates all its opponents, denouncing them as traitors bought with foreign gold, in the same way your future bureaucracy will identify itself with Labour and Socialism and persecute everyone who goes on thinking with his own head, denouncing him as a paid agent of the so-called class enemy.

DON PAOLO (*seized by anger, takes hold of* ULIVA *by his coat lapels and shouts in his face*) But why must that be our destiny? Why can there be no way out? Are we hens cooped up in a hen-roost? Why should we have to remain in the bondage of an unchangeable doom? Why should a State, a society that we want to put at the service of man's brotherhood, be condemned before it has even begun to exist?

ULIVA (*pushing* DON PAOLO *away with a calm and energetic gesture, makes him sit down and for the first time smiles at him in a friendly way*) Come, Pietro, don't let's quarrel. I assure you I didn't come here to argue with you. This is the last time we'll ever see each other, and it would be a pity to part squabbling.

DON PAOLO (*his suspicions aroused*) Why the last time?

ULIVA (*continues without replying*) We've known each other for many years, and in spite of everything I have a certain respect for you. For many years now I've been watching you engaged in a sort of chivalrous joust with life, or with the creator, if you prefer: the struggle of the creature to break down his limitations. All this is very noble; I say it without irony, yes, it is very noble, but it requires a degree of ingenuity in which I am lacking.

DON PAOLO Man has no real existence except in so far as he fights against his own limitations. Man raised himself above the beasts from the moment in which he began this struggle. He turns back into a beast the moment he gives it up; he becomes once more a sheep, or a pig, or a parrot, or a lion, or a hyena, according to temperament, the moment he gives it up. Uliva, we mustn't capitulate. Of course, man is free not to be free; he is free, that is, not to be a man. And it's not easy to be a man. But a man like you, Uliva . . .

ULIVA (*interrupting*) He who finds resignation intolerable and revolution illusory has still one way out that many are afraid of. And yet perhaps it is the only way out that is really worthy of man.

DON PAOLO (*suddenly alarmed*) Uliva . . .

ULIVA (*continuing without taking any notice of him*) You spoke to me once about a secret dream of yours. You expressed it in home-spun language: you would make a Soviet out of the Fucino plain and nominate Jesus Christ president of the Soviet. The idea perhaps mightn't be a bad one if the Son of the carpenter of Nazareth were really on this earth still and could exercise that function in person; but, when the nomination was made and note duly taken of His absence, you would have to find a substitute. And we in this country know how the representatives of Jesus begin and how they end; aye, and don't we know it. The poor negroes and Indians newly converted by the missionaries don't know it, but we know it only too well.

*(The noise of a chair being overturned next
door cuts short the colloquy. A few moments
previously the main door of the inn had opened
slowly and* BROTHER GIOACCHINO *had come
forward in silence. He no longer wears the
Capuchin habit. He is dressed like any poor
old peasant, and is none the less easily recog-
nizable. After making a tour of the room and
glancing at the door in the left wall, as though
he were looking for someone, in walking backwards he inadvertently overturns a chair.* ULIVA
and DON PAOLO *hurry into the wine-shop to see
what is the matter.* BROTHER GIOACCHINO *puts
the chair back into place)*

SCENE 6

The ABOVE, *and* BROTHER GIOACCHINO
(DON PAOLO *and* BROTHER GIOACCHINO *recognize
each other without expressly showing it; each
of them observes the change undergone by the
other; finally the two smile at each other)*

BROTHER GIOACCHINO (*in the slow grave tones of
someone resuming a painful discourse which has been
interrupted*) Then they took up stones to cast at Him;
but He did hide Himself.

DON PAOLO (*with the same tone of gravity and sadness,
and alluding by the fixity of his gaze to* BROTHER
GIOACCHINO'S *loss of his habit*) And He went out of the
temple. Et exivit de templo.

BROTHER GIOACCHINO (*taking* ULIVA *aside with a
fraternal gesture*) You have lost heart because you
think He is here on earth no longer. But I say to you
that He is still here on earth; in hiding, certainly, and

in agony, but on this earth still. As long as He is not dead, we mustn't despair. And perhaps it is for us to see that he is not allowed to die.

(*The* LANDLADY *enters by the door in the left wall*)

SCENE 7

The ABOVE, *and the* LANDLADY

LANDLADY (*to* DON PAOLO) What does your reverence want for supper?

DON PAOLO Anything, except spaghetti.

LANDLADY Soup?

DON PAOLO If you like. But while we're on the subject of soup, padrona, you mustn't mind my telling you something: on my word of honour, I admire your tresses; you really have a beautiful head of hair; but even so, pardon me for saying so, I'm not partial to having too many of your hairs in my soup.

(ULIVA *and* DON PAOLO *leave by the door at the back.* BROTHER GIOACCHINO *remains seated at a table and the* LANDLADY *serves him a bowl of wine and a large slice of bread and then returns to her habitual seat behind the counter*)

BROTHER GIOACCHINO (*dipping a slice of bread in the wine*) Have you had any word of him?

LANDLADY (*indignantly*) Why are you always asking the same thing? You know well enough that he's dead and gone this many a long year.

BROTHER GIOACCHINO You know, you must forgive me, but it's like this, I can't seem to get the notion of his death into my head. Do you remember how full of life he was the time he left for Brazil? I never saw a man as full of life as he was.

LANDLADY Neither did I. And yet he died just the same. After a year was gone, the town clerk came and told me he was dead.

BROTHER GIOACCHINO Had he seen him with his own eyes?

LANDLADY How could he have seen him with his own eyes, and he dead in Brazil? But some kind of paper had come.

BROTHER GIOACCHINO Ah, so you believe in pieces of paper?

LANDLADY (*after a pause*) There's one thing that isn't quite clear. Was it you who turned my husband's head as a boy, or was it he who turned yours?

BROTHER GIOACCHINO (*straining his memory*) Our mothers used to say that the two of us were born with our brains addled. We were born in the same month, the year of the comet, that's how they explained it.

LANDLADY You both had your heads turned, certainly, but not in the same direction. You would have none of the common law either, but you bent your knee to the ancient rule of Saint Francis, poverty, chastity, obedience; whereas he made a special law unto himself, a new standard of right and wrong, and what the authorities find right, he found wrong, and what the authorities find wrong, he found right.

BROTHER GIOACCHINO (*in an undertone*). Perhaps the right way was his way.

> (BROTHER GIOACCHINO *rises to bring the empty bowl back to the counter, and it is only now that the* LANDLADY *notices he is bereft of the habit*)

LANDLADY (*aghast*) Have you run away from the monastery?

BROTHER GIOACCHINO (*in a scarcely audible voice*) The Father Superior turned me out.

LANDLADY Because of what you say about the agony of Jesus?

(BROTHER GIOACCHINO *nods*)

LANDLADY (*overcome with pity*) And how are you going to live now? Do you too want to go wandering the highways and byways and make a special law for yourself different from the ancient law? At your age? Eh, old man, do you too want to end your days lonely and forlorn?

BROTHER GIOACCHINO I spent the whole night turning those very things over in my mind, and this morning at dawn, overcome by weariness, I was on the point of denying Jesus so as to have peace, and I was already on my knees before the Father Superior— when a cock crew.

LANDLADY (*touched*) Listen. You were born in the same month and under the same star as my husband was, you were his companion and friend, and now in the end you've fallen a prey to the same kind of madness as he. If you've got no other shelter, let me tell you this much: your home is here. Don't misunderstand me. (*Entreatingly*) You've no idea what an immense kindness you'd be doing me if you accepted. Because there's nothing sadder than a woman who has an unbounded capacity for devotion and tenderness and never finds a man to lavish it on, or loses him as soon as she's got him, and stays lonely and grows old, weighed down by that measureless force that has no outlet. Listen, old man, think again before refusing me. You've no idea what kindness you'd be doing to a poor woman. And you would lack for nothing, of that you can be certain. You'd be the master here.

BROTHER GIOACCHINO (*after a brief pause*) Is it far from here to Brazil?

LANDLADY There's all the water in the world between here and Brazil, a flood of water, you ought to know that as well as I do. But what makes you ask?

BROTHER GIOACCHINO I could go and find your husband, if you're so fond of him. I could persuade him to come back if you're so fond of him. I've got nothing else to do now.

LANDLADY But he's dead and gone. How many times, bless your soul, must I repeat it? Why do you persist in pouring vinegar into my wound?

BROTHER GIOACCHINO You know, you must forgive me if I keep forgetting it, but as you're aware I don't find it easy to believe in death.

LANDLADY I tell you the town clerk brought me the news.

BROTHER GIOACCHINO Did the town clerk see him dead with his own eyes?

LANDLADY No, bless your soul, no; but he had a stamped paper, and there on the paper was the news.

BROTHER GIOACCHINO Ah, excuse me, I had forgotten that you believe in rubber stamps.

> (DON PAOLO, ANNINA *and* ROMEO *enter by the door at the back; the two latter appear to be deeply upset, almost stunned*)

SCENE 8

BROTHER GIOACCHINO, DON PAOLO, ANNINA, ROMEO

DON PAOLO (*to the* LANDLADY) I shall have two guests for supper.

> (*The* LANDLADY *goes out by the left-hand door.* DON PAOLO *hurries* ANNINA *and* ROMEO *into his*

room and shuts the door. On seeing ANNINA,
BROTHER GIOACCHINO *had gone forward to meet
her, overcome with sudden pity; he now remains
standing for a moment in front of the closed
door of* DON PAOLO'S *room and then goes slowly
over to a seat in the corner of the wine-shop,
makes the sign of the cross and joins his hands
in prayer)*

(The moment ANNINA *enters* DON PAOLO'S *room,
she sinks on a chair and bursts into a torrent
of tears, which she vainly tries to stifle by hiding
her face in her hands)*

DON PAOLO *(terrified, to* ROMEO) What new disaster
are you going to announce to me now?

ROMEO *(utterly dispirited)* Annina will tell you.

*(Her face contracted by spasms of sobbing,
ANNINA tries to articulate a few syllables but
she only succeeds in producing incomprehensible
moans)*

ROMEO *(to* DON PAOLO, *overcoming a growing sense of
dread and pronouncing each word with what is visibly
a painful effort)* Murica has confessed to Annina that
he is a spy in the service of the police . . . That explains
quite a lot of things.

*(There follows a pause dominated by extreme
consternation of the faces of* DON PAOLO *and*
ROMEO *and by* ANNINA'S *sobs, which become
steadily weaker and more tired)*

DON PAOLO *(to himself, in a slow undertone)* That
explains quite a lot of things.

ROMEO I know nothing more. Annina told me
nothing more. Perhaps she will give you some details.

DON PAOLO He has confessed, you said. But why
did he confess?

ROMEO I know nothing more. Annina told me nothing more.

DON PAOLO He knew I was staying here?

ROMEO Yes, of course.

DON PAOLO And why didn't he have me arrested?

ROMEO And me, too, why didn't he have me arrested? He knew where I spent the night.

DON PAOLO I don't understand.

ROMEO There are always obscure inexplicable points in these affairs. I'll leave you two to yourselves.

(ROMEO *passes from the room to the wine-shop and stands in the main doorway looking out at the square.* DON PAOLO *waits for* ANNINA *to speak to him; and since she is silent, he calls her by name, in an undertone, two or three times, in a voice filled with compassion and respect for her desolation; but* ANNINA *remains inert and deaf, with her face hidden in her hands.* DON PAOLO *then opens the window and leans out to scrutinize the surroundings of the inn*)

SCENE 9

The ABOVE *and the* LANDLADY

LANDLADY (*appearing at the threshold of the left-hand door; anxiously, to* BROTHER GIOACCHINO) Are you staying? I'll go and get your room ready this very minute.

(BROTHER GIOACCHINO *breaks off his prayer and shakes his head*)

LANDLADY (*in a voice which is almost that of an angry mother to her rebellious child*) The very wolves have their lairs, and you think the life of a vagabond

72

would suit you better? Who's going to wash your shirt for you? Who's going to heat up your soup for you? Who's going to look after you when you don't feel well? When will you learn sense?

(BROTHER GIOACCHINO *continues to shake his head*)

LANDLADY (*pleadingly*) If you stay here you'll be free to do as you please, you'll be looked up to as the master of the house and you'll want for nothing; and you needn't feel beholden to me either, since it's not for you I'll be doing it, but in remembrance of that man you know of, who was born under the same star as you and was a madman of your own kind, with whom indeed you have much in common.

BROTHER GIOACCHINO (*gently*) I beg and implore you now to understand me rightly, you who were the wife of my friend. If I hadn't come out of a monastery, it's the truth I'm telling you, I'd be glad to stay near you, not as a master, but as a servant. Because you were the wife of my friend, and in serving and honouring you I'd be serving and honouring him too. But you know well enough that I come out of a monastery.

LANDLADY You're not the first.

BROTHER GIOACCHINO I'm not the first. And among those that preceded me, there have been some that eventually settled down in a tavern; but, as to it being any merit of mine, I'm not one of those. I beg and impore you to understand me rightly.

LANDLADY (*angrily*) I understand you and I can't think how it ever came to cross my mind that a man of your sort could be persuaded to do anything sensible.

BROTHER GIOACCHINO (*humbly and sadly*) I see you don't understand me. I'm very sorry for it.

LANDLADY (*suddenly touched*) Of course I under-

69

stand you. And if only I were a man, mark my words, if only I didn't have to wear skirts, I'd follow in your crazy footsteps, and that's God's truth.

> (*She disappears hurriedly inside the door, scared of having perhaps said too much. At the same time* ROMEO *leaves the main doorway and returns to* DON PAOLO'S *room*)
> (ANNINA, *as though awakening, rises to her feet and goes towards the door, taking leave with the tired listless voice of someone who has gone through a great bereavement*)

ANNINA I'm sorry to leave you now when there's so much to be done, but you have others in the movement who can easily take my place.

DON PAOLO (*surprised, catching her by the arm*) Are you abandoning us?

ROMEO (*indignantly*) You're leaving the movement to stay with him?

ANNINA The movement has a great many people; he has only me.

ROMEO But he's so vile, such a repulsive traitor.

ANNINA (*nodding*) And he has only me.

DON PAOLO What is it ties you to him? Pity? Passion?

ANNINA You at least, Pietro, ought to understand. If your brain or one of your lungs or your heart becomes diseased, can you cut yourself free from it? It would certainly be convenient, but it's impossible. You at least . . .

ROMEO You're not even married; you haven't got children; you've never lived together.

ANNINA Those things, Romeo, are certainly important but not really decisive in holding a man and a woman together. Do I have to explain? The really decisive thing, but there's no use explaining this to someone who doesn't feel it, the really decisive thing is when the one feels the other to be no longer a thing outside of himself or herself, but inside, and they are no longer two but one, whatever happens. The horrible, frightful calamity . . . (*She cannot finish the sentence and breaks into sobs*)

ROMEO Can't you see what hell your life with him is going to be?

ANNINA It's going to be hard and difficult, and painful, and lonely; but perhaps not hell; perhaps only purgatory.

ROMEO What sins have you to purge? Why must you take on yourself the expiation of his guilt?

ANNINA Perhaps I must expiate too. If I had shown him my love better, during his last arrest, in prison, he wouldn't have been afraid, he wouldn't have given in just because of the beatings and the vileness of the police.

DON PAOLO And does he accept your sacrifice?

ANNINA No. He argues the way Romeo does. He never wants to see me again. He also wants to make me believe that he doesn't love me any more, that deep down he has never loved me, and that he can't stand my company. But that's not true. In reality he has me in him as I have him in me, and we can never part. He confessed his guilt to me, thinking it would fill me with disgust and drive me away from him; but it is obvious that if he didn't love me he wouldn't have confessed to me and he would have been able to endure the deception.

ROMEO Did you tell him you were going to report his confession to us?

ANNINA Yes.

DON PAOLO And what did he say?

ANNINA I don't know if he understood what I meant. He was terribly overwrought.

ROMEO Is he at home now?

ANNINA I don't know, but I think so.

> (ANNINA *leaves without saying good-bye.* DON
> PAOLO *accompanies her as far as the middle of
> the adjoining room*)

DON PAOLO (*taking leave of her*) We'll see each other
again, Annina. You yourself reminded me the other
day that each of us is responsible for the other.

ANNINA (*deeply moved*) You won't despise me now?

DON PAOLO (*hesitatingly, under his breath*) Annina,
dear Annina, I can't tell you what I think of you now.

> (*They shake hands hastily.* DON PAOLO *stands
> watching her as she goes away*)

BROTHER GIOACCHINO (*to* ANNINA *for whom he is
waiting in the doorway*). I have the same road to go
as you have. Will you allow me to go with you?

ANNINA (*in amazement*). But I don't yet know where
I'm going.

BROTHER GIOACCHINO. Come, I'll show you the way.

> (*They go out*)

CURTAIN

ACT III

The mountain hamlet of Pietrasecca in the Abruzzi Apennines. A bare grey precipitous mountain fills the background; on the summit of the mountain, which is very near and plainly visible, stand three crosses, the middle cross being taller than the two others, which are turned to face it, as in pictures of the Crucifixion. The rest of the stage is occupied by a garden. At the end of the garden where the slope of the mountain begins, there is a spring protected by a few piles of stones: the women of the place go there to draw water. It is late autumn and the garden is bare of flowers and foliage; the black and shrivelled branches of its scanty shrubs resemble twisted wire and strips of metal In the foreground, but still inside the garden, stands a rough stone table, with a bench and two stools. On the left the garden is bounded by a briar hedge, on the right and at the far end by a low wooden fence and by a path; the garden gate is half-way down the fence on the right. The whitewashed façade of a simple little house fills the right-hand side of the stage; between the first-floor balcony and the front door hangs a sign bearing the word INN. The house screens from view the greater part of the village. Outside the door there is a stone bench. A huge pair of bull's horns is fixed to the corner of the house facing the mountain, to ward off the Evil Eye. The stage can be entered not only through the doorway of the inn but also from the right and from the left side of its façade. On the right a path leads up from the valley, on the left another path leads down from the mountain and passes through the village.

SCENE 1

DON PAOLO, ROMEO, CICALA

> (DON PAOLO *and* ROMEO *are in the garden, sitting at the table, which is strewn with books and*

*papers; in front of the inn, where he has left
his cart,* CICALA *is grinding knives and scissors,
his hands, feet and head moving in unison.
A donkey pokes its head out over the hedge on
the left-hand side and gazes, motionless, in the
direction of the garden.* DON PAOLO'S *features
have aged visibly and almost recall a skull;
great dark eye-sockets, hollow cheeks, thin lips
exposing the teeth*)

DON PAOLO No trace of Murica?

ROMEO None. And meanwhile the rounding-up
continues. It appears that anyone they arrest who
won't talk is put to the torture.

DON PAOLO Do you think these last arrests are to be
laid at Murica's door too?

ROMEO Possibly. You know as well as I do that it's
always hard to find out for certain. We're like flies
caught in an invisible spider's wed.

DON PAOLO Is there any news of Annina?

ROMEO Not directly. She has broken off all contact
with us. To be frank, I must say we have every reason
to be disappointed in her.

DON PAOLO Romeo, let's try hard not to be unjust to
Annina: she's a wonderful girl. I had always admired
her. I've known her since she was a child, but I never
dreamed she was so close to perfection. Certainly,
Romeo, it's hard for us men to understand a woman
such as she is, to conceive of a spirit in which our fierce
fanaticism melts away and is transfigured into an
utterly different kind of reality. Even in politics, even
with us, Annina always remained a real woman. She's
fortunate. Women belong to a different world, Romeo.
(*Short pause*) But for the rest I must say I agree with
you entirely. We are men and we must try to be real
men. Where is Annina now?

74

ROMEO She keeps going like a soul in torment, searching for Murica night and day. She's got that unfrocked friar with her, what's his name? Ah, brother Gioacchino. If only Annina had found Murica, it might perhaps have been a kind of protection for us; but as things are, he's a sword of Damocles dangling permanently over our heads.

DON PAOLO Can he still do us such a lot of harm?

ROMEO Plenty. (*Brief pause*) Have you read about Uliva?

DON PAOLO We don't get any newspapers up here. Have they caught him too?

ROMEO Dead. He was blown up together with his wife and children and all the other people in the house, including the caretaker, by the premature explosion of some infernal machine he was preparing in order to assassinate the head of the government. So the papers said, anyhow.

DON PAOLO So he's solved his problem. The last time I talked to him I could see he was meditating some important funeral.

ROMEO (*after a short pause*) And what about yourself, how are you? I don't think the air up here agrees with you any too well.

DON PAOLO I pass endless, sleepless nights. I feel as though I had lived through thousands of years . . .

ROMEO What have you decided to do about Murica? I think we must act quickly.

DON PAOLO . . . thousands of years, Romeo, of torment and anguish: on the border-line between death and madness. (*He covers his face with his hands*)

ROMEO. We've no time to lose about Murica.

DON PAOLO. Romeo, I am not going to give an order for assassination.

ROMEO (*energetically*) Exterminating a viper is not assassination. And there are precedents, as you know.

75

DON PAOLO I shall never give an order for assassination. Not to anyone. Not ever. I can't bear the thought that there should be hired cut-throats or executioners among us: men ready to kill at a mere word of command. (*Pause*) I'm taking it on myself to do away with Murica.

ROMEO (*bounding to his feet in amazement*) You?

DON PAOLO Cicala will just have to find out where he's hiding. I'll take care of the rest.

ROMEO In the state you're in now?

DON PAOLO Believe me, it's the ideal way to be: without hatred and without pity. Like a surgeon. A week ago I couldn't have done it, to-day I can. (*He rises and goes towards the gate*) You'll explain to Cicala that he must hurry with the search.

(ROMEO *stands up to follow him and his glance falls on the donkey*)

ROMEO (*in an undertone, to* DON PAOLO) Do you know that donkey well?

DON PAOLO No, I can't go as far as to say I know him well; I mean we didn't go to school together.

ROMEO Don't you think he's looking at us somewhat suspiciously?

DON PAOLO If you're referring to his ears, you needn't worry; donkeys have always had long ones.

(*They leave together by the gate and take the path leading down to the valley.* CICALA *enters the inn for a moment to return the knives he has ground, then hastens to follow them with his cart. The donkey's head also disappears behind the hedge*)

SCENE 2

The LANDLADY, *three* PIOUS WOMEN

> (*Three women arrive by the path leading down
> from the village. They carry copper and
> earthenware jars and are coming to draw
> water at the spring. They belong to the ancient
> caste of pious women, that is to say, they are
> virgins who have devoted themselves to the
> Church, without giving up domestic life; their
> heads are covered with black kerchiefs, their
> faces are starved and anaemic, they wear long,
> full heavy skirts; their slow and cautious gait
> and their quiet voices are also indicative of their
> way of life. The landlady, as though by pre-
> vious arrangement, comes out of the house, and
> after making certain that the priest is nowhere
> to be seen, she runs to meet them. She is an
> elderly, grey-haired woman, who combines the
> appearance of an ordinary housewife with the
> brisk, free and easy manner peculiar to persons
> who have been for many years 'in business'.
> The only words in the entire conversation that
> are clearly audible are those of the* LANDLADY;
> *the questions and answers of the* PIOUS WOMEN
> *do not rise above a subdued gabble, which in the
> more excited passages distinctly recalls the
> cackling of hens*)

LANDLADY I could get no answer out of him but
this: that he's not from our diocese and that he won't
even hear of such a thing. I tell you he came here with
a letter from Don Benedetto, you know, the parish
priest of Rocca, a friend of his, but he himself is from
another diocese ... The folk that come up here to
see him every now and then just happen to be devout

77

parishioners of his own, he told me so himself . . . To see them coming all the way up here on foot, just to hear his advice, you'd think they were on a pilgrimage . . . He's no ordinary priest, believe me, he's a real saint. At table he scarcely touches a morsel, and for spaghetti he has nothing but contempt . . . Yes, indeed, nothing but contempt for spaghetti, that's as true as you're here . . . He hardly sleeps a wink at night . . . I happen to know that because his room is next to mine, so don't go thinking I peek through the keyhole . . . The fact is, if I were to tell you everything there is to be told, you'd see for yourselves that he's no ordinary priest . . . The way he talks, the way he looks at you, it's not the way of an ordinary priest, that's certain . . . Perhaps he's a saint . . . Saints are always a bit queer, we all know that; indeed it's said they're even a bit mad at times . . . All right, I'll try, I'll try just once more; but you belong to the Church, so you know better than I do what saints are like . . .

> (DON PAOLO'S *reappearance sends the three* PIOUS WOMEN *hurrying away by the path that leads up to the village*)

SCENE 3

The LANDLADY, DON PAOLO

LANDLADY Our poor old church, that hasn't had a parish priest for thirty years, has been cleaned and decorated in honour of your visit. Everyone is rejoicing. It's like when a widow is led for a second time to the altar.

DON PAOLO Have you forgotten that I don't belong to this diocese?

LANDLADY As you repeat it on every possible occasion, I'm not likely to forget it. But even if you

78

do belong to another diocese, we hope that won't keep you from paying our church a visit. When all's said and done, we're Christians too.

DON PAOLO I shall visit the church when I please and I shan't need any gaping crowd of onlookers. I didn't come here on a mission. As I've already told you and as Don Benedetto wrote to you, I came to get a little rest, a little peace. I detest fuss.

LANDLADY The Children of Mary want me to ask you if it would tire you too much to say the rosary with them in church every evening. They're good women, pious women, and it would make them happy.

DON PAOLO I never leave the house in the evenings, as I think you're aware.

LANDLADY As true as I'm standing here, I'd give ten years of my life to be able to boast that a priest of God had recovered his health under my poor roof. So I'll not be the one to pester you in any way. But for the Children of Mary your presence here is a tremendous spiritual event. For years on end, poor creatures, they've been taking care of the church, dusting it and decorating it with flowers; for years on end they've been going there every day, saying the rosary and the litanies, making triduums and novenas, teaching the children their catechism; in fact, doing everything that women are allowed to do when there's no priest. And what's more – I mustn't forget to tell you this – their virtues set a good example and they never fail to take the other women to task, and even the men themselves, whenever they stray from the strait and narrow path. Now these pious and virtuous women may have their faults too, but . . .

DON PAOLO Ah, their gravest faults, it seems to me, are precisely those virtues of theirs.

LANDLADY What do you mean by that? Do their virtues seem vices in your eyes? Strange puzzling words. Do you know, your reverence, I can't get a wink of sleep at night, pondering over certain words of yours?

DON PAOLO Ah, so you were in the habit of using sacred words as sleeping draughts?

LANDLADY The truth is, your reverence, we haven't had a priest here all these years. I'll make so bold as to ask if your reverence is fully aware that our souls are in grave danger. In other parishes the Lord God is a man, a male in fact, but here, speaking with all due respect, He will soon become an old maid. Here in this parish of ours, God's Commandments have now become the commandments of old maids, and the voice of God in our ears is an old maid's voice. I can't tell you how much we suffer from all this. Our religion has been reduced to the state of a barnyard without a cock.

DON PAOLO I'm sincerely sorry for you, from the bottom of my heart, but unfortunately, to use your expression, I'm a cock that already has a barnyard of his own.

> (*A woman, still young, clothed in rags, with dishevelled hair and bare feet, dragging by the hand a little boy about eight years old, comes down the path from the village and goes with a bucket to draw water at the spring*)

DON PAOLO (*to the* LANDLADY) Who is that woman and why does she always go alone to the spring and not in a group, as the others do?

LANDLADY Ever since she lost her reputation no one has talked to her or had anything to do with her any more.

DON PAOLO And when did she lose her reputation?
LANDLADY You see that child she's got with her?

She's not married, so she lost her reputation when the child was born.

DON PAOLO And what about the man? I suppose she didn't produce the child all by herself.

LANDLADY No one knows the father's name.

DON PAOLO Was he a man from hereabouts?

LANDLADY Most likely he was. The woman has never stirred from this place in her life.

DON PAOLO And so even the man will have nothing to do with her?

LANDLADY He may be married and so naturally has his own reputation to think of.

DON PAOLO And the woman never revealed his name?

LANDLADY She refused.

DON PAOLO Out of fear?

LANDLADY No. Out of pride.

DON PAOLO (*quickly*) Did you say pride?

> (*The* LANDLADY *re-enters the house.* DON PAOLO *goes towards the* REPROBATE WOMAN *while she, holding the boy by one hand and carrying the bucket of water with the other, is about to go away*)

SCENE 4

DON PAOLO, *the* REPROBATE WOMAN, *the* CHILD

DON PAOLO (*standing in front of the woman so as to block her path, and smiling at her*) What a beautiful child.

> (WOMAN *puts down her bucket and looks at him diffidently*)

DON PAOLO Can I help you with that bucket?

WOMAN If you only knew who I am.

DON PAOLO And if you only knew who I am.

(*They both laugh*)

WOMAN Have you come to Pietrasecca to say Mass? I'm sorry I'll not be there. But the Children of Mary won't allow me to come.

DON PAOLO. It wasn't to say Mass that I came here. But if I could, I mean if I had the right to say it, I'd say it just for you and your little boy alone, and I'd shut the door so that no one else could enter the church. I would indeed.

WOMAN (*laughing, as though it were a game of make-believe*) And half-way through Mass would you preach a sermon for us?

DON PAOLO Of course, immediately after the Gospel. For instance, I'd preach a sermon on pride.

WOMAN On the vice of pride?

DON PAOLO No, on the virtue of pride.

WOMAN In the meantime, couldn't you ask the Children of Mary to let my little boy attend the catechism class?

DON PAOLO Can he throw stones? Have you taught him to throw stones?

WOMAN No.

DON PAOLO Can he use his fists?

WOMAN No.

DON PAOLO That's bad. There you have the drawbacks of maternal education. Is he plucky?

WOMAN I think so.

DON PAOLO (*taking the boy by the hand*) Come along, I'll teach you to throw stones. First lesson: aim at the legs; second lesson: aim at the head; according to the gravity of the offence.

(*The three disappear round the curve of the*

path in the background: DON PAOLO, *holding the boy by the hand, leads the way; the* WOMAN *follows, carrying the bucket of water and laughing to herself*)

SCENE 5

ANNINA, BROTHER GIOACCHINO

(ANNINA *and* BROTHER GIOACCHINO *arrive by the path leading up from the valley. They both have a long weary road behind them; but while* BROTHER GIOACCHINO *merely looks tired and dusty,* ANNINA *is on the point of exhaustion, and has to lean against the wall of the inn to prevent herself from collapsing. As in the previous act,* BROTHER GIOACCHINO *is without the habit and is poorly dressed, like a labourer; the tonsure, however, is still clearly visible on his bare head.* ANNINA *is wearing an old raincoat and a beret. She sits down on the bench beside the door*)

ANNINA Ah, brother, I can't bear it any longer; I can't bear it any longer; I can't bear it any longer.

BROTHER GIOACCHINO Annina, your heart will give you strength to remain upright to the end.

ANNINA Ah, brother, I'm afraid the end is very near. Believe me, brother, I can't bear it any longer.

BROTHER GIOACCHINO Don't despair, Annina. When you really love, there's no such thing as despair.

ANNINA Ah, brother, the love you know is the divine love of Jesus in His agony, but you don't know the human love of women. My love — brother, you should thank God that He didn't make you a woman — my love is now unending despair.

83

BROTHER GIOACCHINO It's a despair that feeds on hope, Annina, of that I'm certain. Now you rest here awhile. I'll be back immediately.

ANNINA Have we arrived? Is this the place you've been wanting to take me to? What makes you think we'll find him in this part of the world?

> (*While* BROTHER GIOACCHINO *is inspecting the place attentively from all sides, from the garden to the spring,* ANNINA *calls through the inn door, in a strained but quiet voice:* 'Eh! Padrona! Padrona!' *but no one answers. Utterly worn out, she sits down again on the bench beside the door*)

BROTHER GIOACCHINO (*coming back to* ANNINA, *full of pity*) Listen, Annina, I'm used to tramping the roads with my sack over my shoulder, and indeed it's a pretty heavy sack at times; so when you're tired out I could try carrying you on my back. I'd be glad to do it, and I don't think there'd be anything wrong in it.

ANNINA (*with the ghost of a smile*) Poor dear old brother, poor old monk without a monastery, you don't know how much heavier my heart grows every day. It grows heavier and heavier, and soon not even a yoke of oxen will be able to draw it. (*Abruptly*) Do you think Luigi is still alive? Brother, tell me what you think, tell me the truth.

BROTHER GIOACCHINO (*after a pause*) Yes, I think he is still alive, but he's having a great struggle with death.

ANNINA Ah, and to think I can't lift a finger to help him. Brother, what's the good of loving somebody if you can't help him when it comes to the end, and he's struggling with death?

BROTHER GIOACCHINO You know, Annina, I think you are helping him. Listen, Annina, this is much too serious a matter, you know I wouldn't make empty phrases just to console you now. I'm convinced, Annina, that if his soul is still resisting death, it's due to your help alone.

ANNINA But how can you say such a thing, brother, when I don't even know where he's hiding any more than he knows where I am?

BROTHER GIOACCHINO Don't you admit that he loves you very much? And didn't you say yourself that when two people really love each other they grow together, so that each inhabits the other, and they become inseparable? How can you possibly expect the part of you that inhabits him to remain sluggish and indifferent at the very moment when he's struggling with death?

ANNINA (*standing up resolutely*) Thank you for your words, brother, and now let's go, I've rested enough. Where do you think we can find him?

(*The two make their way towards the path in the background while* DON PAOLO *comes down it*)

Scene 6

ANNINA, BROTHER GIOACCHINO, DON PAOLO

ANNINA You here?
DON PAOLO You here?

(*After a moment's hesitation,* ANNINA *follows* DON PAOLO *into the garden and sits down beside him at the table; but their old frankness and cordiality are gone.* BROTHER GIOACCHINO *leaves them and walks over to quench his thirst at the spring*)

DON PAOLO Haven't you found him yet?
ANNINA And what about all of you, have you found him?
DON PAOLO (*diffidently*) We?

ANNINA You're searching for him too, all of you, I've noticed it. Like hounds pursuing their prey. (*With sudden anxiety*) What will you do with him if you track him down?

DON PAOLO (*coldly*) I'm sorry, I'm not at liberty to tell you. You're not with us any longer.

ANNINA (*after a long pause, in a low, stifled voice*) If someone has got to put an end to him – Pietro, let me beg this of you – if someone has to kill him, if that's the way things have been decided, then let it be you.

DON PAOLO (*in amazement*) Me?

ANNINA Yes, Pietro, you would do it without hatred, of that I'm certain. And so the last human image he would see before him and would carry with him into eternity, wouldn't be an image of hatred. (*Entreatingly*) Pietro, if that's the way things have been decided, take this sacrifice on yourself.

DON PAOLO Annina, won't you come back to us? Ah, without you the Party has grown grey and cold.

ANNINA (*rising*) Come back? After what has happened and what is going to happen? Pietro, how could I?

(*She joins* BROTHER GIOACCHINO *who is waiting for her at the corner of the inn, and together they take the path leading up the mountainside.* DON PAOLO *collects the books and papers scattered on the table and goes indoors*)

SCENE 7

The LANDLADY, *the three* PIOUS WOMEN

(*Down the path from the village come the three* PIOUS WOMEN; *one of them has a freshly-bandaged head and is loud in lamentation; the*

86

*others act as chorus, whispering and cackling
around her. The* LANDLADY *hurries out of the
inn to join them)*

LANDLADY He threw a stone at you? . . . The child
of that wretched creature? . . . Jesus, Mary and Joseph,
what is the world coming to? There'll soon be no
religion left if things go on like this . . . No, I wouldn't
call the priest if I were you; he won't interfere, of that
you may be certain . . . Yes, I know the parable too,
the one about the shepherd and the lost sheep, but I'm
sorry to say our priest doesn't like sheep at all, he told
me so only yesterday . . . He prefers cows, just think
of that, cows . . . Holy men often have these queer
streaks . . . What's more, he's got the most peculiar
opinions about vice and virtue, about right and wrong.
I can't get a wink of sleep these nights. . . .

> (*The sound of a stone being thrown and window-
> panes being shattered behind the inn disperses the
> group of* PIOUS WOMEN *who flee in terror,
> shrieking for help)*

SCENE 8

The LANDLADY, LUIGI MURICA
> (*From the left-hand side of the garden, breaking
> through the briar hedge planted on the edge of a
> grassy slope,* LUIGI MURICA *appears on the scene.
> He has the worn, spectral look of a person who
> has been through a serious illness)*

LANDLADY (*from the threshold of the inn*) Hey there,
you, where have you come from?
MURICA From the valley, as you can see.
LANDLADY Were you fishing for trout?

MURICA No, for toads. (*He crosses the garden and approaches the* LANDLADY) There's a priest living here, isn't there? A certain Don Paolo Spada?

LANDLADY He lives here sure enough, but he doesn't wish to be disturbed.

MURICA I must speak to him. Is he in his room?

LANDLADY Do you want to go to confession?

MURICA Well, perhaps that's a good guess.

LANDLADY Which diocese do you belong to?

MURICA What nonsense is this? I don't have to make my confession to you, do I?

LANDLADY The only souls he's interested in are those belonging to his own diocese. The others can go straight to hell, for all he cares.

MURICA But of course, I'm from his diocese too...

LANDLADY H'm. All the same, you speak like one from these parts. What's your name?

MURICA (*showing her a letter*) I've got a letter for him from Don Benedetto.

> (*In silence, like a dense shadow,* DON PAOLO *appears in the doorway of the inn.* MURICA *stands as though rooted to the ground, holding the letter in his outstretched hand*)

•   SCENE 9

DON PAOLO, LUIGI MURICA

> (DON PAOLO *and* MURICA *remain standing for some time motionless, face to face, staring fixedly at each other.* DON PAOLO *appears surprised that* MURICA *is standing up to his scrutiny with so much assurance and without flickering an eyelid*)

DON PAOLO (*in a decided and impatient tone, pointing to the valley path*) Let's walk a pace or two.

MURICA (*not moving*) I want to speak to you.

DON PAOLO (*sternly*) We have really nothing to say to each other. Your idle prating doesn't interest me, and for my part all I have to give you is a brief and curt Party message.

MURICA (*forcing himself to an ironical tone*) A message . . . in my back?

DON PAOLO (*suddenly abandoning all prudence*) If you like to put it that way.

MURICA (*proffering a closed envelope*) Don Benedetto asked me to give you this letter.

DON PAOLO (*sarcastically, leaving* MURICA *with outstretched hand*) So you thought it prudent to come to me armed with a letter of introduction? But it was superfluous, because I know you very well by this time, only too well in fact.

> (MURICA *wants to tear up the letter, but* DON PAOLO *snatches it from him; he then opens and reads it and remains sunk in thought for a while*)

DON PAOLO (*entering the garden, followed by* MURICA) Do you know what the letter says?

MURICA No.

DON PAOLO Have you known Don Benedetto for a long time?

MURICA Since childhood. We're even distant relatives.

DON PAOLO Well, anyhow, please spare me now the tale of the 'heartrending' scene. I know the sort of thing: you went to him, threw yourself at his feet, beat your breast and repeated Mea culpa, wept and confessed. Isn't that what happened? And you finally departed with the firm and pious intention of returning to confess after each new lapse. (*Changing his tone*) Murica, confessors and psychiatrists can allow themselves the luxury of mercy, but a revolutionary

89

party, and you ought to know this much because you have belonged to one, a revolutionary movement, if it's not to betray its mission, in certain cases has got to be merciless to the point of cruelty. Was it Don Benedetto that made you come up here?

MURICA Don Benedetto wanted to have you come to his place, but I preferred to come here.

(*They both sit down at the table*)

DON PAOLO To be frank, I didn't think you so audacious.

MURICA I assure you, it's not exactly audacity. Perhaps it's courage.

DON PAOLO (*stern and aggressive*) Courage? Murica, you're mistaken. A traitor can be foolhardy, rash, imprudent, anything you like, but not courageous. Courage is a peculiar attribute of honesty.

MURICA Perhaps, Pietro, you were born upright, honest, pure and therefore, by nature, also courageous. My courage, on the other hand, if I may be allowed to speak of it, isn't natural; it's always, as in this very moment, a victory over fear: because by nature I'm timid and weak. It's only very recently that I've begun to understand what courage in your sense really is, I mean courage as an aspect of honesty.

DON PAOLO Perhaps you think it courageous honesty to sneak into the trust of your comrades and then betray them to the police?

MURICA My self-denunciation to Annina, at a time when no one even dreamt of suspecting me, was a difficult, painful and supreme act of courage.

DON PAOLO (*after a short pause*) The perniciousness of individuals of your sort lies precisely in this double-facedness, in this inextricable alternation of sincerity and falsehood, good intentions and cynicism, audacity and irresistible, uncontrollable panic. So you confessed everything to Annina, did you? All right; but afterwards? What about the subsequent arrests, the arrests yesterday and this morning? Who was at the bottom of them?

MURICA I don't know. From the day I spoke to Annina I never moved beyond the four walls of Don Benedetto's house. (*Short pause*) I arrived at Don Benedetto's place by sheer accident that very same day. Driven to despair by the irreparable past, I fled across the countryside without realizing where I was going, or by what means I was going there, torn by the feeling that I must commit some bloody act of expiation, suicide for instance, or assassination of some high police officer; when all of a sudden I found myself face to face with Don Benedetto. 'You here!' I exclaimed in surprise; but he had every reason to be amazed at my bewilderment, because without noticing it I had reached a point far up above Rocca, and there I was standing at the entrance to his garden. I wanted to run away, but he held me back and took me into his house. And there he kept me till to-day. Pietro, you know Don Benedetto, because you were a pupil of his for several years, and you know he's not the sort of man to lend himself to the parody of a religious ceremony such as you described a little while ago. And as for me, since the far-off days of my confirmation I've never darkened a church door. If you only knew how much easier I would have found a sacramental confession. Instead, these days I've spent in Don Benedetto's house are going to remain in my life like a painful stay in hospital, like a serious operation. Pietro, you perhaps have never known the real bitterness of evil, nor the dark prison of the irreparableness of evil with never a gleam of hope.

DON PAOLO (*in an undertone, and as though talking to*

himself) The little I know, I too have learned through suffering.

MURICA You know, Pietro, you mustn't think I've come here to act the part of a redeemed, contrite and self-satisfied Magdalen. My soul is still too full of misery. And although Don Benedetto explained and proved to me that no matter how loathsome and detestable evil always is, it's sometimes needed in order that good may spring from it; even though he went so far as to say that, without this almost mortal crisis that I've just been through, I should most likely never have grown to manhood or become mature; nevertheless, this good that I've bought with evil and that I now should settle down to enjoy, this deepened awareness, this belated moral sense, all leave a bitter, disgusting, humiliating taste in my mouth; above all humiliating in the old and true sense of the word, 'prope humo', that is close to the earth, and therefore tasting of worms and putrefaction. Ah, as long as I live I think I shall never lose my horror at this tragic dependence of good on evil: and if I speak of it now it's only in order to add that, compared to this sense of mournful, intimate and lasting bitterness, all my other cares fade into nothingness; even, for instance, my curiosity to know what you intend doing with me.

DON PAOLO To be frank, Murica, if you're being sincere — and I'm trying hard to believe that you are — then I simply don't understand you. What on earth made you come?

MURICA When you've been through hell and you come back to the land of the living, it's your absolute duty to tell others what you've seen. If you go through hell the flames scorch your hair and it stays scorched for ever afterwards, but that mustn't stop you from telling what you've seen. You know,

92

Pietro, the movement of which you are a leader has some alarming aspects that you may not be aware of. Do you remember a passage in an article you wrote recently about a man who by painful degrees becomes aware of his humanity? Romeo gave me that article of yours meaning me to print it; but when I was setting it up in type, that passage stopped me. I could go no farther, and I began thinking.

DON PAOLO You told me that the last time we met in Agostino's stable.

MURICA Now here's the point I'd like you to think over: two years ago when, by sheer accident as you know, I came into contact with the clandestine movement and shortly afterwards joined it, I was incapable of understanding even the literal meaning of those words of yours. In the movement I found myself, consequently, from the very beginning in the position of a gambler staking a much higher sum than he can really afford. If I'm talking like this to you now it's mainly in order to ask you: do you think my case is an isolated one? Don't you think a good many people stake far more than they possess?

DON PAOLO No one ever knows beforehand how much he really possesses. But we're not concerned with other people now. If you felt immature, why did you join a movement full of risks, like ours?

MURICA I think people rebel against the existing order of things for two diametrically opposite reasons: if they are very strong-minded and if they are very weak. By a strong-minded man I mean a man who has risen above the bourgeois order of things, repudiates it, scorns it, fights against it and wants to put a more equitable society in its place. But I was a poor, timid, awkward, lonely, provincial student in a big city; I was incapable of facing the thousand petty hardships of daily life, the little every-day humiliations and

93

rebuffs. I was twenty years old and – forgive me for mentioning this detail – I hadn't yet dared to approach a woman. And that thought kept me far busier and tormented me far more than the future of the world. I realize now that I let myself be drawn into the clandestine movement just because it enabled me to disguise with a proud mask of scorn the resentment I harboured towards the society from which I was shut out, and which nevertheless at the bottom of my heart I envied, longed for and feared. If a weakling rebels against the existing order of things . . .

DON PAOLO In the revolutionary party he can find a virile brotherhood that gives him strength.

MURICA He can also find in it something more convenient. Don't forget that the clandestine form of the revolutionary movement offers a weakling the important and deceptive advantage of secrecy. He lives in sacrilege and shudders at it, but in secret. He stands outside the abhorred and greatly-dreaded law, but that's something the guardians of the law don't know. His repudiation of the established order remains private and secret, as in a dream, and for that very reason it's likely to assume a radical, bloody catastrophical form; but his outward behaviour remains unchanged. In his every-day behaviour the weakling remains as timid, as helpless, as faint-hearted as before. He conspires against the government in the same way that he often strangles his father in dreams at night, only to sit down beside him at breakfast the following morning.

DON PAOLO Until a banal incident reveals his double life.

MURICA Then he's panic-stricken. Terror-stricken.

DON PAOLO (*after some reflection*) Did they beat you when you were in gaol?

MURICA Yes, but I assure you the beatings could add

94

nothing to the fear which seized me ·the moment I was arrested. Besides, my father had often beaten me much more violently when I was a youngster.

DON PAOLO Your father?

MURICA The moment I was arrested I realized I had staked more than I possessed. The challenge I had flung down was out of all proportion to my strength. In giving my personal data I couldn't remember when I was born, nor my mother's maiden name. I signed the statement without reading it. If they had written that I pleaded guilty of robbing and assassinating my grandmother, I should have signed without hesitation.

DON PAOLO They let you out of gaol and then the pangs of remorse began; etcetera etcetera, with all that followed.

MURICA No. As a matter of fact, on my release from gaol I was amazed to discover that I felt not the slightest remorse.

DON PAOLO Not the slightest remorse?

MURICA My satisfaction at escaping so lightly left no room for anything but a vague fear of being found out. I kept asking myself: 'What will Annina say if she discovers my deceit? What will my companions say?' My visit to gaol had considerably enhanced my reputation, and I was terrified of losing it.

DON PAOLO (*sarcastically*) Of course, I quite understand, honour above all.

MURICA But little by little, as I became reassured that it was relatively easy to betray without being detected, my fear of disgrace and punishment began to give way, strangely and unexpectedly, to an increasing horror of impunity. I began to ask myself this question: if a more expert technique of betrayal could guarantee that I should never be found out, would that make evil any easier to bear? I began to find it monstrous that the idea of good should be inseparable from the idea of the useful and linked up with a promise of reward or punishment. So what's useful is therefore good? But useful to whom? To the prisoner anxious at all costs to recover his freedom? To the government party? To the opposition party? To the ruling class? To the oppressed class? And if the idea of good and evil be inseparable from that of reward or punishment – then what is good and what is evil in a society in which virtue is punished and vice rewarded? And if technical competence in the craft of evil were to eliminate all risk of punishment, would this mean the elimination of all distinction between good and evil? In the end, how it happened I don't know, but these reflections left me no peace. My whole being was seized by a new, painful, implacable tension, such as I had never known before. I simply couldn't and wouldn't resign myself to impunity. For many years I had ceased to believe in God, but I suddenly began longing, with all the strength of my soul, for Him to exist. I began to invoke Him, crying into the void. I needed Him urgently in order not to succumb to insanity and chaos. The most frightful punishment imaginable seemed to me infinitely preferable to placid acceptance of a world in which the problem of evil could be solved by a little cunning and dexterity. If I finally decided to confess everything, taking no thought of the consequences, it was with the deliberate and clear-cut intent of setting up order once again between the world and myself, of restoring the ancient boundary between good and evil, without which I couldn't go on living any more. Now . . .

DON PAOLO (*who for some time has been anxiously watching the valley and the mountain path*) Luigi, it's getting late, we'd better go inside. Luigi, thank you for coming. Will you stay here till to-morrow?

MURICA If you want me to. You know, I've still got
a lot of things to tell you.

DON PAOLO I do want you to.

(*They both leave the garden and enter the inn
just as the* LANDLADY *appears in the doorway*)

SCENE 10

The LANDLADY, ANNINA, BROTHER GIOACCHINO
(ANNINA *and* BROTHER GIOACCHINO *arrive by the
path leading down from the mountain*)

ANNINA (*leaning on* BROTHER GIOACCHINO'S *arm so as
not to collapse*) Ah, brother, this time you've got to
believe me, I can't go a step farther, truly I can't.
Please, please, leave me here, or throw me in a ditch,
in a stream, wherever you like; leave me behind and
go on by yourself.

BROTHER GIOACCHINO Annina, that may be a fit
leave-taking for two merchants coming back from a
fair or for two lovers after a ball, but not for us.
Each of us is responsible for the other, Annina.

LANDLADY Have you been on a pilgrimage to the
shrine?

ANNINA (*sitting down on the bench beside the door,
worn out with fatigue*) Yes, on a pilgrimage. We
found the Cross, but not Christ.

LANDLADY Time was, many's the pilgrim came up
here; but in our diocese nowadays the pilgrims would
rather go by train or car to the fashionable shrines that
have hotels with running water. But if you climb up
here you have to sweat, as you may have noticed, and
the running water is in the brook at the bottom of the
valley.

BROTHER GIOACCHINO Anyway, you have a priest
now, they say, a good priest.

G   97

LANDLADY Yes, but he's from another diocese. He won't say Mass or preach sermons and he can't abide the pious women; you'd think they worshipped a different God from his. Penitents from his diocese come all the way up here to visit him, and a queer-looking lot they are. Some of them have the speech of these parts, and yet they must have come from a long way off. You're not by any chance from his diocese too, are you?

BROTHER GIOACCHINO What sort of harvest did you have this year?

LANDLADY If hunger could kill, the folks hereabouts would be in their graves this many a spring. But it's not to refuse you charity that I'm saying this. (*She vanishes into the house and reappears with two pieces of bread and a pitcher of wine*) God sent us pastures, but no flocks, and He sent the flocks to barren fields. He must have His own good reasons, but we don't see them.

(ANNINA *and* BROTHER GIOACCHINO *eat the bread of charity and drink the wine*)

BROTHER GIOACCHINO You know, padrona, somehow I don't think it was really God who shared out the sheep and cows and pigs and horses over the face of the earth.

LANDLADY If it wasn't God, who can it have been?

BROTHER GIOACCHINO You know, padrona, I don't think God was ever a rich husbandman, a man who reared great flocks of sheep and droves of pigs and herds of cattle and horses.

LANDLADY Doesn't God own everything?

BROTHER GIOACCHINO You know, padrona, I don't think God could be in agony on a cross and at the same time own and rear great flocks of sheep and droves of pigs and herds of cattle and horses.

98

LANDLADY (*frightened*) So to your mind, God is poor?

BROTHER GIOACCHINO Yes, I think He is.

LANDLADY Does he too suffer from hunger and thirst?

BROTHER GIOACCHINO Yes, I think He does.

LANDLADY Like any ordinary labourer?

BROTHER GIOACCHINO Much more than an ordinary labourer.

LANDLADY (*terrified*) And what can such a poor wretch of a God, such a down-at-heel God, such a beggar of a God, do to help us?

BROTHER GIOACCHINO He, the Most Holy, can help us, I think, to become still poorer than we are, as poor as He is.

> (*The* LANDLADY *covers her face with her hands to hide her horror.* BROTHER GIOACCHINO *and* ANNINA *rise to leave. The* LANDLADY *notices this only when they are already about to turn the corner of the inn, at the beginning of the path leading down to the valley*)

LANDLADY (*calling after them*) Do you too, by any chance, belong to his diocese?

ACT IV

A large room on the ground floor of a farmhouse, the home of the Murica family in Rocca dei Marsi. The walls are white and bare, the floor is paved with flagstones. The end door, which is flung open and is wide enough to allow the passage of carts, opens on to the yard; there a plough can be seen, with clay sticking to the ploughshare, and a cart with its shaft in the air, outlined against the sky. Above the doorway there hangs a black wooden crucifix and in front of it an oil light is burning in a glass. On the left-hand side of the stage a few stools are grouped in a semi-circle around a burnt-out hearth. A door in the right-hand wall leads to the inner part of the house; two wooden benches are placed against the wall on either side of this door; on the benches stand a pitcher of wine, a few glasses, and a basket of small loaves.

SCENE 1

WOMEN *and* MEN *of the neighbourhood*
(WOMEN *of the neighbourhood, dressed in black and with black kerchiefs knotted under their chins, are sitting on the stools near the hearth:* MEN *of the village, peasants in their dark Sunday clothes, are standing respectfully, cap in hand, near the door in the right-hand wall. Both women and men have come to condole with the family on the death of Luigi Murica. The women of the house can be heard in the adjoining room, mingling low wails with funeral litanies*)

FIRST MAN (*coming in from the yard after the curtain has risen*) Those clerks in the town hall are greatly troubled about the funeral.

SECOND MAN Do the clerks fear Luigi Murica even when he's dead? Do they fear his resurrection?

FIRST MAN The head clerk sent for me to tell me that no inscription will be permitted on the coffin, except of course the name: Luigi Murica, although he didn't think that was really necessary either. He seemed to be greatly worried about the funeral, because of the report he'll have to send in to his superiors afterwards. And what he wanted to worm out of me was this: whether, apart from the name and surname: Luigi Murica – although, mind you, he saw no great need for that either – some spiteful individual might want to disturb folks' peace of mind by writing about how Luigi Murica died.

THIRD MAN Truth needs no inscriptions, it seems to me. If you know a thing already you don't need to see it in print.

FIRST MAN But you know the clerks as well as I do, you know what counts most for them is the inscription. If the inscription is just the usual one, then the death of Murica is just an ordinary death, as far as the clerks are concerned.

THIRD MAN Inscription or no inscription, the dead are in their graves and the living are quick to forget.

SECOND MAN Ah, it'll take more than a few ink-stains to wash the innocent blood of Abel from the earth.

FIRST MAN The head clerk's ambition doesn't fly as high as that. You know him as well as I do, he's a good man, a good father to his children. All that's worrying him is that report he'll have to make.

THIRD MAN He could write that Luigi Murica died of old age at the age of twenty-three, and that would settle everything.

SECOND MAN Come to think of it, when you're dead, the last report of all is written by the worms.

THIRD MAN The last and the same report for every-one: for rich and poor, for clerks and ploughmen, for virgins and swine.

(The FIRST MAN goes out, and the others remain standing in silence)

FIRST WOMAN Was the disaster due to some jealousy among the orators? Maybe the old-fashioned orators couldn't abide his way of talking?

SECOND WOMAN He was no idle talker, but when he thought a thing he wrote it down, and printed it him-self in black and white, on sheets of paper, and then distributed them.

THIRD WOMAN He printed and distributed a sheet of paper and on it was printed in black and white – now I fear I've forgotten it – ah no, now I remember, on this sheet of paper was written: 'Truth and brother-hood shall triumph over lies and hatred.' There were other words too, my husband told me, but I don't recall them now.

SECOND WOMAN The other words were: 'Living Labour shall triumph over money.' It was my hus-band who told me, and I've never forgotten it.

FIRST WOMAN Ah, was he too one of those that have made for themselves a special law, a new notion of right and wrong?

THIRD WOMAN When they arrested him, they found that piece of paper on him and he didn't disown it.

FIRST WOMAN Ah, so he too was one of those.

SECOND WOMAN Then in the yard of the barracks they flouted him in a thousand ways, and the people stood agape at all the nearby windows and on the housetops.

FIRST WOMAN Ah, so he too was one of those.

THIRD WOMAN Then they crowded round him, and put a chamber pot on his head for a crown, and in mockery they said to him: 'This is the reign of Truth.'

FIRST WOMAN The wretches knew not what they did.

SECOND WOMAN Then they put a broom in his right hand for a sceptre, and bowing to him they jeered: 'This is the reign of brotherhood.'

FIRST WOMAN The wretches knew not what they did.

THIRD WOMAN Then they took a red carpet from the floor and wrapped it round him in mimicry of royal purple.

FIRST WOMAN The wretches knew not what they did.

SECOND WOMAN Then they blindfolded him and lashed him to a pillar in the barracks yard.

FIRST WOMAN The wretches knew not what they did.

THIRD WOMAN And the armed men thrashed him and beat him with the butt-ends of their rifles and said to him: 'This is living Labour.' And they taunted him and said: 'Call your companions to come and help you now. Where are your followers?'

FIRST WOMAN The wretches knew not what they did.

SECOND WOMAN When he fell to the ground they trampled on him with hobnailed boots.

FIRST WOMAN And the people stood agape at all the nearby windows and on the housetops?

THIRD WOMAN Finally a scarlet thread of blood began trickling from his mouth.

FIRST WOMAN And the people stood agape at all the nearby windows and on the housetops?

SECOND WOMAN Then they put him on a stretcher — he was unconscious by that time, but not yet dead — and brought him back to his mother and said to her:

'Mother, this is your son, he seems to have had some kind of accident.'

FIRST WOMAN And the people had watched it happen from the windows and from the housetops?

THIRD WOMAN After that he lived on for two more days without recovering consciousness. But before drawing his last breath he opened his eyes and smiled.

FIRST WOMAN O Holy Mother of Sorrows, most merciful Heart pierced by seven swords, intercede Thou for his eternal peace.

SECOND WOMAN Before drawing his last breath he opened his eyes and smiled?

(*A few ancient and tattered* BEGGARS *appear, with hands outstretched, on the threshold*)

SCENE 2

The ABOVE, *with the* BEGGARS *and* DANIELE MURICA

FIRST WOMAN Let them come in.

THIRD WOMAN Maybe they've been sent to spy.

FIRST WOMAN Let them come in. In giving beggars to eat and drink, many have fed Jesus and didn't know it.

(DANIELE MURICA *enters from the adjoining room. He is an elderly grey-haired peasant; his voice and gestures are singularly unhurried and grave*)

DANIELE (*greeting those present with a slight gesture of his hand*) I thank you all for coming. His mother thanks you too. (*He pours out wine and distributes loaves to the* BEGGARS) Take, eat and drink. (*The*

BEGGARS *eat and drink and some of them dip the bread in the wine. To the* WOMEN *crowding round him to offer their sympathy*) Ah, no, I implore you not to say a word. I think, if you'll pardon me, that for such a hideous and unnatural calamity tears would be too frivolous. Perhaps only God, if you'll pardon me, perhaps only God on this occasion has the right to weep. Yes, I have the feeling that at this very moment He is weeping for us His poor creatures. Because He alone can contemplate, without losing His reason, the depths of the abyss of sorrow. And He alone is without guilt. In a case like this our puny reasoning power is like an oil lamp in the darkness and our every-day tears would be of no avail. There, I beg of you, forgive me, don't weep or wail, but eat and drink, you too. (*The* MEN *and* WOMEN *eat and drink*) This is his bread, you know, the bread he can no longer eat. This is his wine, the wine he can no longer drink. The bread that for us now has a taste of ashes. The wine that for us now has a taste of gall. But for each one of you let it be the bread of strength and the wine of healthfulness, and I beseech God, our most merciful Father, to grant my prayer.

FIRST WOMAN And for you and your wife, Daniele Murica, the bread of sympathy and the wine of meekness.

THIRD WOMAN The bread of faith and the wine of charity.

DANIELE Faith and charity; but what about hope? Our earthly hope has been taken from us and we shall grow old in solitude.

THIRD WOMAN Before your son died, Daniele, he opened his eyes and smiled.

SECOND WOMAN He wouldn't have smiled if he hadn't had some kind of hope.

DANIELE Yes indeed, in these last days he confided

to me that hope of his; but we're too old to share it. We'll have to grow old in solitude.

SECOND MAN What sort of new hope is it? We'll have to do with it if there is no other.

DANIELE It is a new hope, based on a new faith and a new charity. But it's not for us, we are too old.

THIRD MAN Is it this strange new notion of good and evil that has been in the air this while past? Was your son another of those that don't believe in the death and resurrection of Jesus, but in His agony?

DANIELE He believed in a new way for people to be together, without fear; a new way for them to help each other and love each other.

SECOND MAN If that's the kind of hope it is, Daniele, there's nothing new about it. When I was a youngster I used to hear my grandfather talk of it, and say it was a fancy of his young days. Of all hopes, I think perhaps it is the most ancient.

DANIELE Well, perhaps it's an ancient hope, as you say. I don't know. The most ancient hope of all, maybe, but founded on a new faith and on a new charity. And for that, as I was saying, we are too old and solitary and distrustful. Ah, you know the way we are. Our hope is no longer of this earth.

(*A* CLERK *appears in the doorway. In appearance he is somewhat of a caricature of the ancient caste of provincial clerks, skinny, wily, foxy, he wears clothes of an old-fashioned cut, with a high, stiff wing-collar, and his pockets are stuffed with papers and official documents. One by one the* WOMEN *and* MEN *take leave of* DANIELE *and go out of the house. Before the* CLERK *begins to speak there comes from the adjoining room a low sound of women wailing and praying*)

DANIELE, *the* CLERK

CLERK (*very uncertainly*) Daniele, I've been sent to you about the funeral. I'm sorry, but the authorities . . .

DANIELE (*interrupting*) Don't let them worry about it any more, everything has been settled already.

CLERK Upon my word, Daniele, I'm very pleased to hear it. As I was saying, I've been sent here to find out exactly what has been settled, and how it has been settled.

DANIELE Don't let it worry you. I repeat, these are family matters.

CLERK Why of course, Daniele, the funeral expenses are borne by the family. But the authorities desire that on the coffin, apart from Christian name and surname . . .

DANIELE There'll be neither Christian name nor surname on the coffin. What would be the use? Everyone will know who is in the coffin and how he came to be there.

CLERK I'm glad to find you so reasonable, Daniele. Now about the hearse being accompanied to the graveyard . . .

DANIELE Don't let it worry you, it has been settled already. The mourners will naturally follow the hearse just as they always do.

CLERK Now listen to me, Daniele, I've been asked to inform you that it is forbidden to follow the hearse to the graveyard.

DANIELE I'm sorry, but I see you've been wrongly informed. The neighbours and relatives will naturally accompany the hearse, just as they always do. That has been settled already and there's no use in talking about it.

CLERK (*threateningly*) A law-abiding man like you can't go against the authorities, Daniele.

DANIELE Certainly not; but if two authorities disagree, which of the two should one obey?

CLERK What do you mean by that, Daniele, if two authorities disagree? I don't understand your riddles.

DANIELE How can I explain? Look here, when you were a soldier, if the corporal gave you one order and the lieutenant another, whom did you obey?

CLERK The lieutenant, that goes without saying. But that is completely beside the point.

DANIELE And if the lieutenant gave you one order and the colonel gave you another?

CLERK The colonel, of course. But that's enough now, Daniele; kindly explain . . .

DANIELE Thank you. And if the colonel gave you one order and the general gave you another?

CLERK (*out of patience*) The general, Daniele, the general, that goes without saying; but now that's quite enough, and will you kindly explain from what higher authority you claim to have received a countermand?

DANIELE Must I really name Him? I'm amazed that you can't guess Who it is.

CLERK (*peremptorily*) There's no authority but one in this country now, Daniele, you understand? One, and one alone. And he rules over everyone and over everything. You shouldn't forget that.

DANIELE Everything? It seems to me that for all your learning, you've used the wrong word this time. (*Pause*) For how long, would you say, have there been families in the world? I'd like you to answer that one.

CLERK Daniele, I didn't come here to be cross-questioned by you.

DANIELE Please answer me.

CLERK According to the Bible, for six thousand

years, according to science . . . But I tell you, Daniele, I didn't come here to be cross-examined by you.

DANIELE Just so, and six thousand years ago the whole business of being born and dying was settled once and for all. That was before the time of this government of yours. And after it has vanished from the face of the earth, people will go on being born and dying in accordance with that old unchangeable law, the law of families. Of course, the powers that be can kill a man; they can decorate and reward the assassins. It's not at all hard to kill a man. But once a man dies, his soul belongs to God and his body belongs to his family. That has been settled once and for all. How long ago did you say it was that families began?

CLERK (ill at ease) Well, and what answer am I to take back to my superiors?

DANIELE You can say that I've already paid my taxes.

CLERK And about the burial?

DANIELE You can say that when you got here you found that everything had been settled already. Settled quite some time ago. And if they insist on knowing exactly how long ago it was, you can say: about six thousand years. Isn't that about how long there have been families?

CLERK And you don't think the authorities are likely to intervene with force?

DANIELE It would be a bit late.

CLERK Why late?

DANIELE Everything has been settled already. How long ago did you say it was that families began?

CLERK Daniele, don't you think the authorities are likely to use force to prevent the people from accompanying the hearse to the graveyard?

DANIELE Of course, everything is possible, even the worst sacrilege; but then?

CLERK What then?

DANIELE The quarrel will cease to be between you and me, poor weak old man that I am; and it will become a quarrel between you and . . . You know to Whom I am alluding. I don't name Him because I know He doesn't like being named in vain. I shouldn't like to be in your shoes when that happens.

(DANIELE *leaves the* CLERK *and goes into the adjoining room.* PIETRO SPINA *and* BROTHER GIOACCHINO *enter from the yard.* SPINA *has resumed lay clothing and his appearance is in every way identical with that of* ACT I)

SCENE 4

CLERK, PIETRO SPINA, BROTHER GIOACCHINO

SPINA (*to* BROTHER GIOACCHINO, *pointing to the* CLERK) Isn't that creature one of the clerks we saw talking in front of the town hall a little while ago? (*To the* CLERK, *in a threatening tone*) What are you doing here, you wretch? How could you dare?

(SPINA *takes hold of the* CLERK *by his coat-lapels and pushes him violently against the wall, but* BROTHER GIOACCHINO *separates them*)

BROTHER GIOACCHINO Leave him alone; he's an old acquaintance.

CLERK (*straightening his necktie and coat and darting terror-stricken glances at the two strangers, alternately squinting at the door out of the tail of his eye*) I've never had the honour. Are you sure we've met before?

BROTHER GIOACCHINO So you consider the possession of records a dispensation to forget?

SPINA When we saw you talking and gesticulating a little while ago, together with your wretched accomplices, brandishing your papers with the brazen assurance of card-sharpers, it almost seemed to me that your were conscious of a certain repetition.

CLERK On the contrary, my dear sir, the motive of our meeting was altogether exceptional. We were examining the legal aspect of this unfortunate and painful incident, and trying to find some way of bringing all these agitated people back to their senses.

BROTHER GIOACCHINO Ah, how many times in the course of the centuries have you uttered those very words, on the evening of the day on which an innocent man was impaled or burned or crucified?

CLERK In the course of the centuries? You're joking. I'm barely forty-five years old.

(CLERK *is seized with a fit of nervous convulsive laughter*)

BROTHER GIOACCHINO Your ignominy is much more ancient than you are.

SPINA If you were only forty-five years old your perfidy would not be so great.

BROTHER GIOACCHINO (*to* SPINA) You were asking me a little while ago where I had heard the horrible news. I was going down towards Rocca, and at the crossroads before you come to the mill I caught sight of an old woman a little way off, surrounded by a few shepherds. The woman wasn't shouting nor making a fuss of any kind, her hands were crossed on her breast and, as far as I could judge from that distance, she barely moved her lips as she spoke; the men were bending forward a little to catch her words, they were as still as statues and their faces were the colour of lead. I recognized that ancient scene the moment I beheld it, and all of a sudden, for horror and pity, my heart stopped beating. It was in that very way, in the suburbs of Jerusalem, about two thousand years ago, in the first week after

111

the first full moon of spring. It was in that very same way that the news of Our Lord's crucifixion was spread.

CLERK The way you talk about it, one would think you had been there yourself.

BROTHER GIOACCHINO Perhaps you've forgotten it, but you were there too, wretch that you are. We were all there.

CLERK Me too?

BROTHER GIOACCHINO Of course you were. Together with your worthy colleagues, you were worried about the legal aspect of the painful incident, and you were trying to think of soothing words to calm people down and make them forget.

(*All of a sudden the* CLERK *grows pale and clutches the air with his hands, as though about to faint.* SPINA *has to support him in order to prevent him from collapsing on to the floor; the moment he recovers, he casts one glance around him and takes to his heels in terror. In the doorway he almost collides with an* OLD RELATIVE *who is coming to pay a visit of condolence.* DANIELE *comes forward to meet him from the adjoining room; they greet each other and embrace without a word. A little later* ANNINA *also enters by the door in the right-hand wall. The presence of* SPINA *and* BROTHER GIOACCHINO *escapes her notice at first*)

SCENE 6

PIETRO SPINA, BROTHER GIOACCHINO, DANIELE MURICA, *an* OLD RELATIVE, ANNINA

OLD RELATIVE (*to* DANIELE, *pointing to* ANNINA) Who's she?

DANIELE She was his fiancée. His fiancée from the

town. (*To* ANNINA, *in an effort to comfort her*) Did they tell you that he smiled? Before breathing his last, he opened his eyes and smiled.

ANNINA He that could never smile for joy?

DANIELE Perhaps he was smiling at that hope of his.

ANNINA Ah, what a sad destiny, if joy was always to mean suffering for him, and if he had to wait for death to be able to smile without remorse. (ANNINA *discovers the presence of* SPINA. *In tones of bitter reproach:*) Pietro, you promised to go away; your imprudence in coming here is beyond belief.

SPINA (*embarrassed*) We'll be leaving in half an hour. Brother Gioacchino and I wanted to bid you good-bye.

DANIELE (*observing* SPINA, *whom he does not yet know*) Where are you from?

SPINA From Orta.

DANIELE What was your father's name?

(ANNINA *murmurs a name in* DANIELE'S *ear*)

DANIELE (*with a gratified smile*) I knew your house when I was a lad. At a cattle market I once sold your father a mare of mine. I've heard tell of you from my son who has been taken from me. (*To* ANNINA) Did you know each other long?

SPINA When I first knew her, she still wore her hair in pigtails. We used to call her 'Sparrow', she was so shy.

ANNINA It was he that taught me to fly.

SPINA (*to* ANNINA) Ah, if only I had known that you would have to pay for it with so much suffering.

OLD RELATIVE (*in amazement*) To fly? (*Flapping his hands to imitate the flight of a bird*) Really to fly?

SPINA (*smiling*) Shall I teach you too?

DANIELE We are too old and heavy and earthy and the joints of our bones have rusted.

OLD RELATIVE And there are too many hunters lying in wait for those who fly.

(DANIELE *pours out wine and breaks bread and offers it to those present*)

DANIELE Take, eat and drink. This was his bread. This was his wine. And they will be sustenance for him no longer.

(*The three visitors eat and drink; the* OLD RELATIVE *dips the bread in the wine*)

SPINA Bread is made of many grains of corn. That's why it means communion. Wine is made of many grapes, and it too stands for communion. Community of similar, fraternal, useful things; things that go well together.

BROTHER GIOACCHINO But before they can come together the corn has to be ground in the mill and the grapes have to be trodden in the winepress.

DANIELE Nine months are needed to make bread.

BROTHER GIOACCHNIO But first of all the corn has to be ground in the mill.

ANNINA Nine months?

DANIELE In November the grain is sown, in July it is reaped and threshed. (*He counts the months on his fingers*) November, December, January, February, March, April, May, June, July. That makes nine months. Grapes, too, need nine months to ripen, from February to October. (*He counts the months on his fingers*) February, March, April, May, June, July, August, September, October. That makes nine months too.

BROTHER GIOACCHINO But first of all the grapes must be trodden in the winepress.

ANNINA Nine months? I'd never thought of that.

OLD RELATIVE The same time as it takes to make a man.

DANIELE And to unmake him, it takes so little.

BROTHER GIOACCHINO No more than it takes to grind in the mill or to tread in the winepress.

(DANIELE *leads the* OLD RELATIVE *into the adjoining room*)

ANNINA (*taking* BROTHER GIOACCHINO *aside*) Brother, you promised me to accompany Pietro to the city and never to leave him and to help him in all his needs and to be father and brother and friend to him. And you'll feel yourself responsible for him, won't you?

BROTHER GIOACCHINO I'll do my best, but you know what he's like.

ANNINA Brother, you promised me. When are you leaving?

BROTHER GIOACCHINO Any moment now. Cicala is coming with a horse and trap to fetch us.

SPINA So you're plotting against me, eh? What cowardice, two against one.

(ANNINA *is called away into the next room. The three peasants of the first scenes of* ACT I, AGOSTINO, DONATO *and* MATTEO, *follow one another in from the yard, uncertain and hesitant*)

SCENE 6

PIETRO SPINA, BROTHER GIOACCHINO, AGOSTINO, DONATO *and* MATTEO

AGOSTINO (*to* DONATO *and* MATTEO) Come on now, come along in, you two. You've kept me company this far, and you're not going to leave me in the lurch now, are you?

SPINA Agostino, you here? What on earth are you doing?

AGOSTINO (*in astonishment*) Well, I came, or rather we came, hoping that someone in this house could help us to find you again.

SPINA Find me? What for?

(MATTEO *recognizes* BROTHER GIOACCHINO *and, noticing that the latter no longer wears the habit, he makes gestures of admiration*)

AGOSTINO I came, or rather we came, to talk to you. I mean to take up again that conversation of ours, I don't know if you still remember it, the conversation that day in my stable. Now Donato can explain the rest.

DONATO (*to* AGOSTINO, *retreating*) You've started, so you may as well continue. Or did we come here to stand on ceremony?

AGOSTINO (*to* DONATO) The idea of coming here was yours and now that we're here it's only fair that you should be the one to explain your idea.

MATTEO Begging your pardon, Agostino, you're right in saying that it was Donato's idea to begin with, but we've made it our idea now; now it belongs to all of us here, and to others that are not here to-day, and that you know of, and that we can name. It's not just one man's idea any more.

AGOSTINO (*to* DONATO *and* MATTEO) Well, if I get it mixed up you'll put me right. When all's said and done, there's no need of so many words, it seems to me. (*To* SPINA) You told us, if I remember rightly, that you had come back from foreign parts to bring us together. You said that a man is truly a man only if he has a feeling of brotherhood for other men. Well,

116

at that first meeting, as I fear you'll remember, our answer to you was no; but now we've made up our minds. Donato would have explained it better, but that's the point of it.

(BROTHER GIOACCHINO *smiles to himself*)

DONATO Well, there's no more to be said. We've thought it over, and we've made our choice. That's all. There'll be no turning back, and there'll be others – we can tell you their names – that have promised to be with us.

SPINA (*trying not to show his delight*) Do you realize what a dangerous path you're taking?

MATTEO We've turned everything over in our minds, and we have chosen.

SPINA You know what happened to Luigi Murica?

AGOSTINO That's why we're here.

DONATO A carter brought the news down our way yesterday evening.

AGOSTINO After hearing the news Donato called a crowd of us together and said to us: If we don't unite now, if we don't put ourselves together, infamy will settle down in our lands, like cholera, like leprosy, like malaria in the marshes.

DONATO (*to* SPINA) What we should like to know is this: do you think it's too late?

SPINA Without you, perhaps it would have been too late. But the fact that you're here now is proof of the contrary. Your coming has given me a secret hope.

AGOSTINO You must explain to us what we are to do and how we are to begin.

MATTEO You must guide us.

(*A sound of clattering hoofs and jingling reins precedes the appearance of* CICALA *in the door-way at the back*)

The ABOVE, *and* CICALA

CICALA (*to* SPINA *and* BROTHER GIOACCHINO) Let's be off, everything is ready for the journey.

SPINA Cicala, you must forgive me for having asked you to make all these preparations, because they're of no use now. No use whatever. We're not leaving after all.

> (BROTHER GIOACCHINO *takes the dumbfounded* CICALA *aside to inform him of what has happened*)

SPINA (*to* AGOSTINO, DONATO *and* MATTEO) Well, here I am at your disposal. At last.

DONATO We have found you a good hiding-place in a part of the country where they're not likely to hunt for you.